Edinburgh Review
Introductions to Scottish Culture

R.D. Laing

R.D. Laing

Gavin Miller

Edinburgh Review
in association with
Edinburgh University Press

© Gavin Miller, 2004

Reprinted in hardback, 2005

Edinburgh Review, 22A Buccleuch Place, Edinburgh
in association with
Edinburgh University Press Ltd
22 George Square, Edinburgh

A CIP record for this book is available
from the British Library

Pb ISBN 1859332706
Hb ISBN 0748622578

Printed and bound in Great Britain by
Antony Rowe Ltd., Chippenham, Wiltshire

Contents

Acknowledgements

I would like to acknowledge the support and assistance of the following individuals and institutions. For their support and editorial vision, Cairns Craig and Ronald Turnbull. For access to the R.D. Laing collection, Glasgow University Library. I also thank the following for their generosity in reading and commenting upon the manuscript of this book: Daniel Burston, Karina Dent, Colin Kirkwood, Tom Leonard, and Ronald Turnbull. For his assistance in providing an image of R.D. Laing, I thank John Duffy.

Chapter Four is based upon the article 'Cognition and Community: the Scottish Philosophical Context of the "Divided Self,"' published in *Janus Head* 4.1 (Spring 2001). An earlier version of Chapter Five appeared as 'The Democratic Psyche: Scotland's Philosophical Psychiatry' in *The Irish Review* 28 (2001).

Abbreviations

A	Erving Goffman, *Asylums: Essays on the Social Situation of Mental Patients and other Inmates*
AP	Thomas Szasz, 'Anti-Psychiatry: the Paradigm of the Plundered Mind'
AT	Jeffrey Masson, *Against Therapy*
AV	Marius Romme and Sandra Escher, *Accepting Voices*
BC	W.R.D. Fairbairn, 'Reevaluating Some Basic Concepts'
BMI	Thomas Scheff, *Being Mentally Ill*
BS	John Macmurray, *The Boundaries of Science*
CD	*R.D. Laing: Creative Destroyer*, ed. by Bob Mullan
CE	Daniel Burston, *Crucible of Experience*
C22	Joseph Heller, *Catch-22*
D	Dorothy Rowe, *Depression: The Way out of your Prison*
DI	George Elder Davie, *The Democratic Intellect*
DM	René Descartes, *Discourse on Method*
DOS	Philip Thomas, *The Dialectics of Schizophrenia*
DS	R.D. Laing, *The Divided Self*
DSM	*Diagnostic and Statistical Manual of Mental Disorders*, 4th edition
EI	David E. Scharff and Ellinor Fairbairn Birtles, 'Editor's Introduction: Fairbairn's Contribution'
ESC	Craig Beveridge and Ronald Turnbull, *The Eclipse of Scottish Culture*
FJ	J.D. Sutherland, *Fairbairn's Journey into the Interior*
FL	R.D. Laing, *The Facts of Life*
FM	Elaine Showalter, *The Female Malady*
FO	Wilhelm Reich, *The Function of the Orgasm*
GL	David Cooper, *The Grammar of Living*
GP	Karl Jaspers, *General Psychopathology*
I	Thomas Szasz, *Insanity: The Idea and its Consequences*
IE	John Macmurray, *Interpreting the Universe*
IHP	Dorothy Heard, 'Introduction: Historical Perspectives'
IP	R.D. Laing, H. Phillipson and A.R. Lee, *Interpersonal Perception*
IPl	Erving Goffman, 'The Insanity of Place'
JM	John E. Costello, *John Macmurray: A Biography*
K	R.D. Laing, *Knots*
LM	David Cooper, *The Language of Madness*
LRS	W. Robertson Smith, *Lectures on the Religion of the Semites*
MC	Herb Kutchins and Stuart A. Kirk, *Making Us Crazy*
MCi	Michel Foucault, *Madness and Civilization*

MMI   Thomas S. Szasz, *The Myth of Mental Illness*
MTBN   Bob Mullan, *Mad to Be Normal: Conversations with R.D. Laing*
OL   F.A. Jenner, 'On the Legacy of Ronald Laing'
OLH   Ian D. Suttie, *The Origins of Love and Hate*
PAP   David Cooper, *Psychiatry and Anti-Psychiatry*
PC   Maxwell Jones, *The Process of Change*
PE   R.D. Laing, *The Politics of Experience*
PF   R.D. Laing, 'The Politics of the Family'
PH   Rudolf Bultmann, 'The Problem of Hermeneutics'
PP   Peter Sedgwick, *Psycho Politics*
PR   John Macmurray, *Persons in Relation*
PS   Erving Goffman, *The Presentation of Self in Everyday Life*
RAC   Ron Coleman, *Recovery: An Alien Concept*
RDL   Adrian Laing, *R.D. Laing: A Life*
RDL-DS   John Clay, *R.D. Laing: A Divided Self*
RDL-PAP   Zbigniew Kotowicz, *R.D. Laing and the Paths of Anti-Psychiatry*
RDL-PV   Bob Mullan, *R.D. Laing: A Personal View*
RF   Wilhelm Reich and A.S. Neill, *Record of a Friendship*
RMI   Martin Roth and Jerome Kroll, *The Reality of Mental Illness*
RP   W. Ronald D. Fairbairn, 'A Revised Psychopathology of the Psycho-
           ses and Neuroses'
RPD   Judith M. Hughes, *Reshaping the Psychoanalytic Domain*
RS   Gwen Howe, *The Reality of Schizophrenia*
RV   R.D. Laing and D.G. Cooper, *Reason and Violence*
SA   John Macmurray, *Self as Agent*
SS   Thomas Szasz, *The Second Sin*
SSD   Mary Boyle, *Schizophrenia: A Scientific Delusion?*
SFP   W. Ronald D. Fairbairn, 'Schizoid Factors in the Personality'
SHN   J.B. Baillie, *Studies in Human Nature*
SMF   R.D. Laing, *Sanity, Madness, and the Family*
SO   R.D. Laing, *Self and Others* (1st edition)
SOf   W. Ronald D. Fairbairn, 'The Treatment and Rehabilitation of Sex-
           ual Offenders'
S5   Kurt Vonnegut, *Slaughterhouse-Five*
THN   David Hume, *A Treatise of Human Nature*
TP   Peter R. Breggin, *Toxic Psychiatry*
TR   R. Lifton, '"Thought Reform" of Western Civilians'
UAP   Lucy Johnstone, *Users and Abusers of Psychiatry*
VE   R.D. Laing, *The Voice of Experience*
WM   Daniel Burston, *The Wing of Madness*
WMF   R.D. Laing, *Wisdom, Madness, and Folly*

WN   W. Ronald D. Fairbairn, 'The War Neuroses – Their Nature and Significance'

WS   Gwen Howe, *Working with Schizophrenia*

W7   Valeriy Tarsis, *Ward 7: an autobiographical novel*

Introduction

The psychiatrist Ronald David Laing, born in 1927, was possibly Scotland's most important public intellectual of the twentieth century. When he died, aged 61, on 23 August 1989, memorial services were held in London, New York, and other cities across the world. During the twentieth century in Scotland, perhaps only the educationalist A.S. Neill (1893–1973) comes close in fame and influence. Currently, Laing's work and ideas (like those of Neill) are neglected in his home country, and the Scottish intellectual culture which preceded and surrounded him is largely forgotten. There is no Laing Institute of Human Relations; no university holds a chair of psychiatry in his name; no plaques mark the places he was born and educated.

In the course of his life, R.D. Laing moved from the forefront of humane, and humanist, psychiatry to a position of notoriety. Latterly, he was alcoholic, professionally unlicensed, and as disturbed, at times, as anyone he had ever treated. His work also descended into near-madness – he implied, for example, that his problems could be traced to the hostility of his mother's uterus, eight days after he was conceived. It is hard to forget such a figure; but it is easy to overlook the radical challenge to psychiatry of his earlier work and ideas.

Much attention could, instead, be paid to the psycho-biographical aspects of Laing's life. He seems to have been raised in the kind of family he would later come to regard as conducive to schizophrenia. However, though this upbringing gave Laing a motive and material for his theories, it did not give him the intellectual skills to analyse his own experience. For those, we must turn to his education, his training, and his dialogue with his peers. The aim of this book is therefore to explore the depth, validity, and context (both national and international) of Laing's work.

For some, this effort will seem misplaced. Laing, they will say, was a charlatan and a self-publicist, and if his name is no longer familiar to us, then it is deservedly so. Such instant dismissal, indeed, is a threat which faces all thinkers who oppose conventional psychiatric practice. There is a stigma of irrationality which is frequently attached to anyone who seems to criticise the authority of psychiatric science – as if medical investigation were, indeed, the only way to reasonably apprehend the world. This book will show, though, that there are many good reasons why conventional psychiatric diagnosis, care, and treatment may be challenged.

Laing, furthermore, is doubly disadvantaged. Not only does he criticise a complacent scientific establishment, he also comes out of a nation which has, of late, shown little interest in its culture. Indeed, to many Scots, there may even be little sense of an ongoing intellectual life in their country. I first encountered Laing's ideas as a teenager interested in natural sciences and planning to study astrophysics. I read an interview with him in a (now-defunct) US popular-science magazine. Here was something even more extraordinary than artificial intelligence and black holes: here was a public intellectual who was clearly taken seriously, was certainly Scottish … and whom I had never heard of before in my life.

A decade and a half after my first encounter with Laing's work, as a postdoctoral academic in literary studies, I attempted to fund a conference on it, to be held in an old and renowned Scottish university on the seventy-fifth anniversary of his birth. The plan was stymied: according to a senior academic at the prospective host university, Laing 'warts and all' was 'too warty.' Laing, in his later years, published some bad books, drank too much, lost his professional reputation, and had a tendency to violent outbursts. This much may be said, I suspect, about less well known scholars and academics, and is small beer compared to the quirks of other, more celebrated intellectuals: the German existentialist Martin Heidegger (1889–1976) professed his faith in the Nazi Party, and the French philosopher Louis Althusser (1918–1990) throttled his own wife to death. Yet, Laing's latter decline is taken as reason enough to neglect what is valuable in his work. The French and the Germans would never be so uncharitable towards one of their own thinkers, but then they are not small countries dominated by a state centred in a larger and indifferent neighbour.

Surely, though, one should not link national and intellectual life in this way? A culture of ideas which is narrowly national is not a genuine intellectual culture; great ideas arise in international contexts. Nor should a nation dictate to its thinkers what their thoughts should be. Ideas are important because they are thoughtful, well-argued, and profound – not because they are Scottish or English or Danish or Estonian.

Yet, though nations are primarily defined by the boundaries of a certain level of governmental power (the state, usually), they also have secondary functions. Intellectual life can receive a national dimension because nations allow investment (in the broadest sense) in programmes of research; and where these programmes are typical we may speak of a national movement (British empiricism, American pragmatism – perhaps, even, Scottish psychiatry). In an 'ideal world,' these intellectual tribes would never need to appear. Ideas, though, are formed not in an ideal world, but in a reality where original research may appear at first glance to be nonsense, and where hypotheses are proven after years of argument, not accepted before the first article is published. Universal rational consensus is an ideal, and an indispensable one, but hardly ever a reality; nations may allow space for new ideas to develop and grow, rather than to be weeded-out because no one has yet seen these strange plants mature.

Perhaps, then, we have the second reason for Laing's marginal intellectual status: there is little institutional support or sympathy for his ideas in Scotland. To note the absence of such support is not to call for an unthinking worship of Laing in the spirit of 'my country, right or wrong;' it is, though, to ask for a more charitable recognition of his work than has hitherto been provided in his homeland.

A begrudging attitude to Laing's achievements is perhaps particularly Scottish, is probably recent, and is, I hope, reversible. It is, though, quite real, and it is also a sign of a more general complacency and forgetfulness. When I first encountered Laing's work, I was a school student living in Burntisland, a small Fife town, to which I had moved with my parents after earlier living in Forfar, a town just north of Dundee. I attended a high school in Kirkcaldy which took in pupils from the smaller towns in the area. For each of the three towns – Kirkcaldy, Forfar, Burntisland – there was a locally neglected intellectual. Adam Smith (1723–1790) is world famous as the founder of modern economics, yet there were few signs of his relation to Kirkcaldy, where he wrote *The Wealth of Nations*. It may be that Forfar in some way recorded the birth of A.S. Neill, the anti-authoritarian educationalist who did so much to liberate education in Europe and the US from Victorian repressiveness. As I recall, though, his teachings seemed largely to have bypassed the local schools. Burntisland also had its own neglected figure: the nineteenth-century astronomer and mathematician Mary Somerville (1780–1872), who was famous in her own day, and to whom Somerville College, Oxford, owes its name.

In the square where Mary Somerville's house still stands in Burntisland, there is an architectural metaphor for the recent condition of Scottish intellectual life. Across from the idiosyncratic, yet traditional, form of Somerville's house are a series of functional concrete flats and houses built over the rubble of houses much like Somerville's during a period of post-War civic 'regeneration.' In the name of improvement and progress, the architectural past was largely erased; perhaps only because of the Somerville connection, were a few of the old houses preserved.

Such architectural destruction hints at the need for an archaeology of Scotland's intellectual heritage. Laing is an obvious case of this neglected history. Too much basic work on his ideas has remained undone within Scotland. Laing's papers are preserved in Glasgow University Library, and his autobiography *Wisdom, Madness and Folly* was republished by Canongate Classics in 1998, but there is little direct scholarship being conducted on his work in his home country. Furthermore, the context that he arose from, one of Scottish philosophers and psychiatrists, needs still to be clarified and examined.

Yet, athough Laing's ideas are not particularly celebrated in Scotland, his thought has undergone something of a revival in North America. Two scholarly books on Laing by Daniel Burston – *The Wing of Madness* and *The Crucible of Experience* – were published in 1996 and 2000 to significant acclaim and interest. Also, in 2003, The Society for Laingian Studies was formed by a group of interested individuals in order to promote and sustain interest in Laing's work. It may be that enough time has lapsed so that one may take from Laing's ideas what is valuable, discarding what is less useful.

This book, then, tries to reconstruct the meaning of Laing's ideas as they arose in his time, and to put them into the scattered fragments that remain of the cultural context from which he emerged.

The first chapter concisely outlines Laing's remarkable life. Though my focus is on his ideas, the events of Laing's life cannot be neglected. Laing rose from a lower middle-class household in Glasgow in the

1930s to a position of international intellectual celebrity, from which he then declined into notoriety and drunkenness during the 1970s and 1980s

Laing, though he may have had few obvious Scottish peers, was not alone in his criticisms of conventional psychiatry. Across the world during the 1960s, intellectuals and writers were beginning to regard sceptically the value of institutionalisation, the reality of mental illness, and the validity of therapy. This field of ideas, which came to be known as 'anti-psychiatry,' is the subject of my second chapter. 'Anti-psychiatry' was generated by thinkers such as Erving Goffman, Thomas Scheff, Thomas Szasz, and David Cooper, and by writers such as Valeriy Tarsis and Ken Kesey.

In the third chapter, I discuss Laing's contribution to this movement. Laing was not a systematic thinker, but his work shows a continuity in ideas, and frequently revolves around the problem of a life lived without feeling. From his central concerns, radiate various approaches, some dwelling on the interior intelligibility of madness, others on the role of social relations, and some on the way experience is stifled by social constructions.

Laing rarely referred with any gratitude or respect to his education in Scotland. Yet, before and beside Laing's ideas is a rich context of Scottish philosophy which shows striking affinities to his work – especially to his analysis of the 'divided self.' My fourth chapter discusses in particular the ideas of the twentieth-century philosopher John Macmurray, who is perhaps the only Scottish philosopher Laing explicitly mentions in his published work. Macmurray's ideas resonate with those of Laing both as an influence, and as a parallel, philosophical theory.

Macmurray's ideas harmonise not only with those of Laing, but also with those of two twentieth-century Scottish psychotherapists, Ian Suttie and W.R.D. Fairbairn. The fifth chapter discusses the work of these two thinkers. During the 1930s, Suttie (to whom Macmurray refers) criticises the premises of traditional Freudian psychoanalysis and challenges the reality of mental illness. Fairbairn advances similar arguments, and is explicitly acknowledged as an influence by the US anti-psychiatrist, Thomas Szasz.

I conclude with a chapter which examines the continuing challenge to mainstream psychiatry by the movement today known as 'critical psychiatry.' On the one hand, critical psychiatry challenges the medical tendency to scientifically explain and categorise supposed 'mentally ill' behaviour. On the other, it demands recognition and understanding of those who are stigmatised by a psychiatric diagnosis because, for example, they hear voices, or engage in some other behaviour incomprehensible to medical specialists. In many ways, critical psychiatry continues the project to which Laing contributed so much.

2002 marked the 75th anniversary of Laing's birth. It is a peculiar fact that, had Laing been a more successful human being, he would probably now be an even more neglected figure. Such is the complacency of Scots towards their own intellectual heritage, that the work of quietly respectable thinkers is readily forgotten. Laing's later life of notoriety, though, cannot be smothered by the usual cultural amnesia. Those who care to look into Laing's ideas will find insight and candour; and beyond that, an unfamiliar context of psychiatric and philosophical ideas developed by Dr Jekylls who had no Mr Hydes to ensure their lasting memory.

Chapter One

Life

Ronald David Laing was born in Govanhill, Glasgow on 7 October 1927 to David Park MacNair Laing and Amelia Glen Laing (neé Kirkwood). David Laing was an electrical engineer with the local Electricity Board; Amelia was a housewife. The couple met when David was in the RAF during World War I; at the time of Ronald's birth, they had been married for ten years. The event was a surprise to friends, family and neighbours. Amelia Laing had concealed her pregnancy, and even denied having had sexual relations with David (RDL 23).

A family where such denial could occur, as might be expected, was not necessarily a happy environment. Although the Laings were well-off, and so spared the poverty endemic in the nearby Gorbals, both David and Amelia engaged in rather bizarre behaviour. Because of a long-standing family dispute, David Laing seems regularly to have come to blows with his own brother (FL 10). He also, when Laing was a teenager, had a three-month breakdown precipitated by uncertainties in his career. Behind such events, lay David's relationship with his own father, 'Old Pa,' whom he regarded as having oppressed his mother; indeed, David's words to Ronald on the death of 'Old Pa' were 'Now the bastard's dead' (WMF 83). Laing recalls his father's breakdown: 'He had started to tremble, inexplicably. [...] For most of the three months he lay in bed' (WMF 83). David's breakdown involved an unfounded belief that he would be passed over for promotion by his boss. Laing, however, saw this reaction as a guilty projection of 'Old Pa' onto his father's employer: 'I told my father that I thought it was very unlikely that his chief Inglis was trying to do him in. [...] It was Old Pa, his father, that it must be all about' (WMF 84).

Laing's mother was still more psychologically peculiar. According to one friend and neighbour, 'Everyone in the street knew she was mad' (RDL-DS 7). The Laing family home was frequently curtained and dark; and, as if to avoid contamination by the outside world, Amelia 'was rarely seen outside her house. She even burnt her own rubbish at home, lest neighbours found what it contained' (RDL-DS 8). Daniel Burston

records other evidence of Amelia's oddities: 'on the rare occasions when
Amelia travelled downtown with the boy, she took lengthy detours
around certain districts of Glasgow in order to avoid the malign influence of people living there who were hostile to her' (WM 12). Amelia
Laing was undoubtedly, because of her own peculiar experiences, unable
to deal with raising a son. Burston's summary is apposite: 'on some very
deep level, Laing was not a wanted child. At the same time apparently,
Amelia felt constrained to behave in ways that conformed to prevailing
cultural expectations of what a mother *should* feel toward her offspring'
(WM 11). A key example was when Amelia gave her five-year old son an
expensive pedal car. This token of maternal love, however, was issued
only after she had burned his previous toy, a much loved wooden horse,
on the grounds that he was excessively attached to it. Another rather
vindictive strategy was to circumscribe her son's private tastes and extra-
familial relationships. This involved a careful policing of his diet, lest
Laing should consume improper foods which might mark his communion with the lower sort of people – jam and jelly babies seem to have
been particularly annoying contaminants for Amelia. Her peculiar
behaviour continued into Laing's teens. In what seems like a ritual that
evolved into a spot check for masturbation, Amelia would interrupt her
child bathing (which he did daily) in order to briefly clean his back. This
practice ended when Laing, aged fifteen, locked the door, while his
father foiled Amelia's protests by threatening to make a scene which
would alert the neighbours (WMF 59–60). These incidents show
Amelia's problems in relating to her son, and the difficulties that must
have faced Laing in attempting to both win her approval and live independently. And, although Laing's relationship with his father was more
amicable, the latter colluded with Amelia's behaviour, and must also
have set rather a disturbing example of violent masculinity.

  Against this background, even the post-war Scottish educational system must have seemed liberating. Laing thrived at primary school, and
blossomed at grammar school. He was academically outstanding (with
the exception of maths), a capable sportsman, and an extremely accomplished young musician. Laing also employed Glasgow's municipal
facilities. He later recalled that he read the Danish existential philosopher Kierkegaard 'in the reference library that was just across the back
green from where we lived. The Govan Hill Public Library. […] I was

looking up the card index and I was working my way from A to Z'
(MTBN 93). In October 1945, Laing entered Glasgow University to
study medicine. His course consisted of 'one year of physics, chemistry,
botany and biology. One year of anatomy and physiology. Then the clinical years of general medicine, surgery and the other major divisions of
orthodox Western medicine' (WMF 73). Laing seems to have thrown
himself into university life with an incredible vigour. As well as a sheer
love of learning, he had an ambition to achieve intellectual significance:
'I had to put in the groundwork now to give myself a chance later [...] of
being in a position to make any possible "contribution" of any moment
or substance in any field' (WMF 73). Laing, in emulation of his academic
masters, began to cut down on sleep, hoping to achieve more with just
two or three hours a night. This intense scholastic existence was also
combined with extra-curricular activities. As well as climbing and drinking with the Mountaineering Club, Laing founded a philosophical
debating society, the Socratic Club, and successfully asked Bertrand
Russell to be its president.

Laing also exercised the sceptical spirit which was later so manifest in
his work. He protested at the use in lectures of 'films of prolonged X-
rays of the body, showing joint movements, and movements of the
digestive tracts, peristalsis, etc.' (WMF 74). These were films created by
Nazis during World War II; the subjects were Jews who were killed by
the prolonged radiation exposure necessary to record the images.
According to Laing, such rebellion against the system also explained his
failure to pass his medical exams: during the final-year dinner, he was
'sitting beside the senior professor' and 'said some things that were
definitely out of order' (MTBN 49). Adrian Laing, though, suggests an
alternative explanation: 'Ronnie's spectacular fall from grace was due to
the absence of any foundation in science and his obsession with extra-
curricular interests' (RDL 42). Whatever the explanation for this failure,
it had one, probably rather happy consequence. Laing was so annoyed at
his parent's sense of disgrace that he abruptly left home, and would
hardly ever return. He passed his medical examination six months later,
in December 1950, and graduated in February 1951 (RDL 43).

Laing then worked until September 1951 at the Neurosurgical Unit in
Killearn near Glasgow. There he met a neurosurgeon, Joe Schorstein,
whom he would later describe as 'my spiritual father, neurological and

intellectual mentor, and guide to European literature' (WMF 92). Schorstein, a Jewish refugee, had 'met Jaspers, Heidegger, and Buber,' 'had walked out of a lecture by Alfred Adler,' and 'was a master of the European tradition' (WMF 93). Schorstein intensified Laing's contact with Continental literature and philosophy, and provided a personal link to great European thinkers. Laing, however, was not destined to enter the tradition of European existential psychoanalysis. The story of this foiled ambition is related in Laing's autobiography:

I corresponded with Karl Jaspers, the Swiss psychiatrist-philosopher. He agreed to 'take me on' once a week to begin with, and to arrange for me to attend the Neuropsychiatric Department at the University of Basel [...]. I was given a scholarship through Glasgow University to study with him in Basel. Then the British Army extended their dragnet to include my medical grade. I went before a board in Edinburgh who determined that I would serve 'the cause' better by putting in two years in the British Army. (WMF 95)

At the end of Laing's period in Killearn, he therefore entered basic training for the Royal Army Medical Corps. Afterwards, he was posted to the British Army Psychiatric Unit in Netley, near Southampton (RDL 47–48). There he encountered first-hand the practice of insulin comas. Patients were put into deep coma with insulin, and then recalled from death by glucose solution fed into the stomach. Electric shocks were also employed upon patients. The rationale for both procedures seemed to be the same: 'The brain is chemically poisoned in some way and the mind is full of unintelligible gibberish. Wash it out, wipe it, clean the brain, and cleanse the mind' (WMF 99–100). Such well-rationalised dehumanisation had its counterpart in the everyday conduct of certain staff. Laing was confronted with a patient who had, it seemed, delusions of being beaten up in the middle of the night. When these beliefs spread to other patients in a case of '*folie à quatre*,' (WMF 101) their truth could not be denied; courts martial soon followed. Netley also gave Laing opportunities to develop his skill in the comprehension of patients. Against the prevailing ethos, he spent time alone with patients, attempting to enter into their world and understand their speech and actions. Laing even took a patient home with him on leave to Glasgow. There he advised this individual to display no symptomatic behaviour on his return to Netley: 'If he could not keep up that much, I could not guarantee that I could save him from electric shocks and maybe a diagnosis of schizophrenia and deep insulin before he could get out – and then, almost certainly, only to a civilian mental hospital' (WMF 107).

After a year at Netley, Laing was transferred to Catterick Military Hospital in Yorkshire. It was while in Yorkshire that he married his first wife, Anne Hearn. They had been in a relationship in Netley; it was while Laing was in Catterick, though, that he received a letter telling him she was six months pregnant. They were married in October 1952, but Laing's parents did not attend the wedding (RDL 50–51). The marriage was not happy, and deeply frustrating for Laing. He had held out hope of rekindling his relationship with Marcelle Vincent, a Parisian who had been his girlfriend while on exchange study at Glasgow University. Now that hope too was dashed.

Laing returned to Glasgow in late 1953, and took up a post at Gartnavel Royal Mental Hospital. There, in the 'refractory' ward, he befriended a patient who was occasionally admitted for manic episodes. She was his guide into the meanings expressed by the seemingly intractable cases: 'she told me that a patient, for instance, huddled in the far corner of the ward, gazing fixedly out a window, was furious that I had not looked at her when I had entered the ward. That patient curled up under a table, she told me, had been playing at being a snake for years' (WMF 123). These observations lead Laing to propose an experiment – the 'Rumpus Room.' Eleven 'schizophrenic' patients were selected, and given access on weekdays to a large comfortable room with materials for various pastimes; later, a stove and oven were provided for tea-making and baking. Soon, the patients 'were recognizably ordinary human beings again, however daft they were' (WMF 126). A further consequence intrigued Laing: 'Within eighteen months all original eleven patients had left hospital. Within a further year, they were all back' (WMF 126). Was it perhaps the social environment outside the hospital which drove these patients to madness? This possibility would be explored in Laing's later studies of family and social context.

In 1956, with the completion of his Diploma in Psychiatric Medicine, Laing formally qualified as a psychiatrist (RDL 59). He soon moved to London with his expanding family in order to train as a psychoanalyst at the Institute of Psycho Analysis. He had been headhunted by a fellow Scotsman, John D. Sutherland, Medical Director of its parent organisation, the Tavistock Clinic. As well as the usual academic tribulations, training required a four-year analysis with an established practitioner (RDL 62). Laing's approach to this experience was undoubtedly somewhat inauthentic: he wanted to graduate as a psycho-analyst, and would do whatever was necessary. Nevertheless, despite his strategic approach to his own analysis, and irregular attendance at lec-tures, Laing's talents were recognised. When attempts were made to delay Laing's qualification, one staff member argued that an exception should be made for this 'specially brilliant student' (RDL-DS 68). Laing's analyst, Charles Rycroft, was also generous in his praise: 'Dr Laing is by far the most intelligent candidate I have yet had in analysis or supervision and has more than an average feel for the unconscious, and he thinks for himself' (WM 53).

Laing, though, was sceptical of his training. He would later say to Bob Mullan that 'from very early on at the beginning at the Tavistock I felt sort of "fuck this," I had really fucked myself up here' (MTBN 149). He was cut off from the extreme psychotics he had encountered in Gartnavel, and was only partly at home in the intellectual climate. Although he had conceptual affinities with Winnicot, Rycroft and others, he was uncomfortable with the theories of Melanie Klein. In particular, he regarded Klein as likely to indulge in reductive interpreta-tion of opponents: 'it was simply impossible to disagree with her. She would simply say take that up with your analyst, for analysis. "Your ana-lyst will give you a personal interpretation of how you want to suck his penis or rip off her nipple, which you are displacing onto me."' (MTBN 160). Laing also had troubles beyond his professional life. In 1959, his closest friend, Douglas Hutchinson, died in a mountaineering accident (RDL 65). His marriage to Anne was also disintegrating. In 1960, the strain of these events seems to have overwhelmed Laing. He suffered a mysterious illness and, according to Adrian Laing, 'nearly died' (RDL 67).

Despite these trials, though, Laing was beginning to achieve a measure of professional success. His first book, *The Divided Self*, was published in 1960 by Tavistock Publications, and was followed in 1961 by *Self and Others*. Laing qualified as a psychoanalyst in 1960 and set up a private practice in London. He was soon introduced to LSD, and began (with Home Office permission) to use it for therapy. His career at the

Tavistock Clinic was also taking off. With Aaron Esterson, Laing was conducting studies into the families of schizophrenics; this empirical work would be published in 1964 as *Sanity, Madness and the Family* – the same year as *Reason and Violence*, Laing's introduction to Jean-Paul Sartre (co-authored with David Cooper). Laing's commitments during this period were intense. As well as the usual course of research and administration, he lectured, wrote popularising articles, travelled widely, and began to make radio and television appearances. Laing was also motivated by a desire to escape his failing marriage. Indeed, in 1963, he briefly moved out in order to live with a lover. Although he later returned, his marriage would continue to disintegrate, and effectively dissolved in 1965, when he took up with Jutta Werner, a young graphic designer, with whom he would eventually father three children. Laing's first wife and her five children, after an abortive attempt to live in France, returned to Glasgow in 1967.

In 1965, Laing joined with David Cooper and Aaron Esterson to form the Philadelphia Association – an organisation inspired by experiments such as the Rumpus Room, and Cooper's Villa 21, a unit for young 'schizophrenics.' The Association obtained premises, Kingsley Hall in London, and opened their community in June 1965. Kingsley Hall would have many residents attracted by its liberal regime, which was unwilling to proscribe the deviant behaviour of the mad. The most famous of these was Mary Barnes, who would later publish an account of her extreme regression and consequent recovery. At one point, records John Clay, 'she performed a sundance naked on the roof, covered in her own faeces, and anxious neighbours rang up the fire brigade' (RDL-DS).

Kingsley Hall, probably to its detriment, soon became something more than a therapeutic establishment: 'Young Americans [...] fresh from reading *The Divided Self* [...] took a taxi straight from the airport and arrived, expecting to be let in and allowed to stay' (RDL-DS 131). Laing would later summarise his own feelings to Bob Mullan: 'I thought to myself that Kingsley Hall was certainly not a roaring success. But it is providing lessons that we can learn from *anything*, even if it simply shows that this particular way of doing it is not the way it is going to work' (MTBN 190). The mythology of R.D. Laing was beginning, however: the rumour at the time was, recalls Laing, 'I was mad, *or I was dead*. I heard quite a number of times that I was a ruined, tragic figure, who had fallen into the clutches of my own profession and been wiped out with electric shocks' (MTBN 192).

At the end of 1966, Laing moved out of Kingsley Hall. He went briefly in early 1967 to the William Alanson White Institute of Psychiatry, Psychoanalysis and Psychology in New York, where he spoke on 'inter-personal aspects of the understanding and treatment of schizophrenia, the family context, and the use of LSD in a formal therapeutic setting' (RDL 129). In 1967, *The Politics of Experience* and *The Bird of Paradise* were published, further consolidating Laing's role as a prominent counter-cultural figure. As Adrian Laing aptly puts it, '"R.D. Laing" was becoming a byword for a whole system of ideas, the central theme of which was a challenge to the recognized order' (RDL 134). Laing was soon lecturing alongside the Marxists Lucien Goldman and Herbert Marcuse, and the black power activist Stokely Carmichael. Some of Laing's broadcasting work in 1968 also appeared in print. His 'Massey Lectures' for the Canadian Broadcasting Corporation were published in 1969 as *The Politics of the Family*. Laing also used the late 1960s to complete *Knots*, a popularising poetic exposition of his work on interpersonal relations. This was eventually published in 1970.

The end of the 1960s prompted Laing to retreat from his demanding schedule and from the pressures of fame. He mothballed his private practice, and made plans to travel to Sri Lanka and India. Accounts of Laing's time in these countries are vague, and it is hard to distinguish reality from self-promoting myth. The bare facts are clear enough, and summarised by Burston (WM 117–20). Laing was out of the United Kingdom from March 1971 to April 1972. He stayed first in Sri Lanka, and then in India. His fundamental aim was to meditate. He worked by himself, and also under the guidance of others. Perhaps the most exotic experience was his three-week stay with the guru Gangotri Baba, which eventually led to Laing's initiation into the cult of Kali. Burston records that on Laing's return to London, he was 'relaxed, refreshed and in splendid health' (WM 120). Within several months, though, Laing had resumed his bad habits. Furthermore, financial mismanagement soon forced him to go on a whirlwind American lecture tour which precipitated a physical collapse.

Laing's therapeutic approach also took an unusual turn in the 1970s. He became fascinated with rebirthing therapies, and eventually conducted group rituals based around this practice. The most charitable interpretation of this therapeutic approach compares it to shamanism, and argues that Laing had moved beyond orthodox psychiatry into ritual practices ignored and marginalised by Western culture. Whatever the efficacy of these *rites-de-passage*, the accompanying analysis was weak. The corresponding volume, *The Facts of Life* (1976), is one of Laing's most implausible efforts. Perhaps the real problem was desperation. As Burston notes, not unfairly, Laing's 'creativity was dwindling as his books became increasingly self-referential' (WM 129). Whatever the motivation, Laing's involvement with this practice inevitably diminished his credibility even amongst previously sympathetic colleagues.

The late 1970s held other difficulties for Laing. In 1976, Susie, Laing's second child by Anne, died of leukaemia. Furthermore, David Laing's health was steadily declining. Since the late 1960s, he had been the victim of worsening Alzheimer's disease. Despite the difficulties in their relationship, it was undoubtedly traumatic for Laing to see his father in this condition. In *The Facts of Life*, he recalls the effect of discussing his father's ailing health: 'my eyes fill with ears, they well up, run over, run down my face,' 'my tongue and facial muscles are heaving incoherently' (FL 82, 83). David Laing died 21 April 1978.

Laing's professional existence in the 1980s continued to be somewhat fallow. His primary publications were *The Voice of Experience* (1982) and his partial autobiography *Wisdom, Madness and Folly: The Making of a Psychiatrist* (1985). Although both books were superior to *The Facts of Life*, and show a revival of cogency in Laing's work, they had rather disappointing sales. Laing's personal life was also very troubled during this time. In 1981, his marriage to Jutta disintegrated, and he began various other relationships (fathering his ninth child *en route*). Laing eventually found stability again with his secretary, Marguerite Romayne-Kendon, towards the end of 1984. She lived with Laing until the end of his life, and together they would have his tenth child in 1988.

Marguerite compelled Laing to sober up in the late 1980s. However, prior to this, much of his wild behaviour continued, and seems to have been particularly marked in the period between Jutta and Marguerite. Bob Mullan provides some vignettes from this time. On 23 May 1984,

Laing attended a conference on shamanism in California with the title 'Awakening the Dream: the Way of the Warrior:'

Bored with the formal proceedings Laing visited a bar and began howling at the moon. The regulars in the bar believed he was making fun of them, a fight ensued and Laing received cuts and a black eye. The following day Laing claimed, in his terms quite accurately, that he was a high priest of the goddess Kali. An American shaman asked him to renounce Kali, beating him with a shovel as he did so. Laing's shoulder was dislocated but he bore no hard feelings toward the man. (RDL-PV 177)

There are further tales from this period of drunkenness, brawling, and even of assaults on residents in Philadelphia Association communities (see WM 136–39).

On the other hand, Laing was still capable of extraordinary displays of psychiatric comprehension. One well-recorded incident occurred at a psychotherapy conference in Phoenix, Arizona in December 1985. Laing arranged to conduct a live interview with a diagnosed paranoid schizophrenic. The interview was held in private but transmitted to the conference audience by closed-circuit television. Unexpectedly, the interviewee asked to join Laing in the main auditorium, where she took questions and exhibited no abnormal behaviour. This occasion, notes John Clay, showed Laing's ability to conduct 'an unscripted meeting between two people, each risking to take on the other' (RDL-DS 239). This capacity was absent, it would seem, in some of the audience – one of whom even effectively referred to the woman (in her presence) as a 'zombie' (RDL-DS 238). For her part, the young woman declared of Laing, 'I think this guy would be a great psychotherapist' (RDL-DS 239).

Two pivotal events appear in what may been seen as the final decline of R.D. Laing. Both were legal matters, and are described well by Adrian Laing, Laing's son by Anne. Adrian Laing was a criminal barrister, and assisted his father during both cases. The first was Laing's conviction in 1984 for possession of a small amount of cannabis. The case was sparked by an incident in September 1984 in which Laing threw a bottle through the window of a Buddhist centre in London. He was searched after his arrest and a quantity of cannabis resin was found. Laing's conduct in the subsequent police interview was not helpful to his case.

Adrian Laing records how his father arrived drunk, and was eventually sent home on the understanding that 'if Dr Laing again turned up drunk he would be detained in the cells until he had sobered up' (RDL 216). Adrian dissuaded his father from defending a plea of not-guilty. On 27 November 1984, Laing's case came before the court, which sentenced him to a twelve-month conditional discharge.

A year later, Laing came to the attention of the General Medical Council. In December 1985, a patient complained about an incident which occurred during treatment in 1983. The patient alleged that Laing had been drunk during consultations, and had also invited him take a drink as well. Although this complaint was eventually dropped, the GMC continued to question Laing's suitability to practise on two grounds. The first was the cannabis conviction. The second was a 1985 radio interview with Anthony Clare as part of the latter's series, *In The Psychiatrist's Chair*. Laing had admitted in this interview to severe depressive spells and to the abuse of alcohol. Adrian Laing sardonically summarises the evidence with which the GMC questioned Laing's fitness as 'a withdrawn complaint, a spent conditional discharge for 6.98 grams of hashish and the transcript of a public interview with Professor Anthony Clare' (RDL 228). Rather than dispute their claims, Laing instead chose a deal whereby he voluntarily removed his name from the Medical Register. So it was that on 20 May 1987, Laing ceased to be a medical practitioner.

By that time, Laing had also endured the loss of his mother, who died on 10 November 1986. On receiving the news, he played the Victorian song, 'A Boy's Best Friend is His Mother' (RDL-DS 247), in a duet with his friend Theodor Itten. During the service, which was conducted in Glasgow, Laing began to cry uncontrollably. As hostile as Laing may have been to his mother, his empathy for the disturbed undoubtedly arose from his relationship with her – a relationship whose effects he perhaps never quite outgrew. One mourner recalled that 'he was still three years old in relation to her, his rage still there' (RDL-DS 247).

Two years after his existential 'death' as a medical practitioner, came Laing's physical end. For several years he had suffered from steadily increasing rectal bleeding, and even giving up alcohol could do little against what was probably rectal cancer. The proximate cause of Laing's death, though, was cardiac arrest. In 23 August 1989, while with friends in St Tropez, he died of a heart attack during a tennis match. A funeral service was conducted in Glasgow Cathedral, and in January of the succeeding year, a memorial and thanksgiving service was held in St James', London.

If there was one common theme in the obituaries which followed Laing, it was this, as recorded by Daniel Burston, 'they all praise *The Divided Self*, Laing's first book, and lament the decline in creative power that seemed to follow on his increasing infatuation with fame' (WM 145). This undoubtedly reflects a fair judgement on Laing's work: the demands and temptation of playing the role of guru took him away from the thoughtful clinical and philosophical research which he could perform so brilliantly. However, despite all Laing's personal failings, he wrote perceptively on many vital issues. He also opens a window onto the neglected intellectual life of Scotland. He was born and educated in Glasgow, and learned in a rich context that included not only Anglo-American and Continental luminaries, but also Scottish philosophers and psychiatrists.

Chapter Two

Anti-Psychiatry

R.D. Laing's work has often been regarded as part of a movement which flourished during the 1960s. At that time, in Europe and North America, there developed a varied scepticism towards conventional psychiatric diagnosis, care and treatment. This movement came to be known as 'anti-psychiatry' – a term popularised by the psychiatrist David Cooper in *Psychiatry and Anti-Psychiatry* (1967). In the English-speaking strand of anti-psychiatry, Cooper and Laing were central figures, but one might also include the psychiatrist Thomas Szasz, the sociologists Erving Goffman and Thomas Scheff, and writers such as Ken Kesey. All were sympathetic to individuals who suffered because of a psychiatric diagnosis.

The term 'anti-psychiatry,' however, is rather a clumsy label. Szasz vehemently refuses it, and Cooper came to regret ever having invented it. Laing himself was also unhappy with the term. Nonetheless, the label has stuck. It should not be taken, though, to imply that 'anti-psychiatrists' were wholeheartedly against diagnosis, care, or treatment; the majority, in fact, sought to critically revise (to varying degrees) established psychiatric practice. They did argue, however, that conventional psychiatry was insensitive to the rights of patients and the potential intelligibility of their condition. In this sense, Cooper, Laing, Szasz, and others, were 'against' psychiatry.

Erving Goffman and Thomas Scheff

Erving Goffman was born in Alberta in 1922. After studies in chemistry and sociology in Canada, he pursued postgraduate research in the University of Chicago. His doctoral work was conducted in Scotland, where he was attached to the Department of Social Anthropology at the University of Edinburgh. Goffman studied the interaction of residents in the Scottish islands, where he found inspiration for his theories on self-presentation. This work lead to his first significant publication, *The*

Presentation of Self in Everyday Life (1959), originally issued by the
University of Edinburgh Social Science Research Centre in 1956. His
own work may well have been influenced by his personal circumstances:
his wife (whom he married in 1952), suffered from 'mental health' problems, and committed suicide in 1964. Goffman died in 1982, by which
time he was one of the most influential of North American sociologists.

In *Asylums: Essays on the Social Situation of Mental Patients and Other
Inmates* (1961), Goffman applies his theories to the 'mentally ill.' His
essays report his research into the world of the inmate – and particularly
the mental patient – as he or she experiences what Goffman refers to as
the 'total institution.' Like prisons, army camps and monasteries, mental
hospitals are places cut off from society, where a homogenised group of
people lead a regimented life which is bureaucratically administered in
many aspects. Like army conscripts or prison inmates, mental patients
are also confronted by a superior social caste (in their case, doctors,
nurses, and warders) by whom they are observed and disciplined. Much
of Goffman's analysis concerns the effect of total institutionalisation
upon the patient's sense of selfhood. In particular, he concludes, much
of what is seemingly 'mental illness' is a way of withstanding the total
institution. This is why 'the craziness or "sick behaviour" claimed for
the mental patient is by and large a product of the claimant's social distance from the situation that the patient is in' (A 121).

Goffman's interpretation begins in his keen sense of the haphazard
path to hospitalisation for 'mental illness.' Anyone who can circumvent
the chain of events that leads to hospitalisation can avoid being locked
up. As he wryly remarks, 'in the degree that the "mentally ill" outside
hospitals numerically approach or surpass those inside hospitals, one
could say that mental patients distinctively suffer not from mental illness, but from contingencies' (A 126). For those who are unlucky,
though, there begins a stripping away of their selfhood. Trusted loved
ones may encourage the eventual patient to surrender his or her liberty.
They and medical professionals sweeten the unpalatable truth, leading
the agent further and further into the role of a mental patient deprived
of the 'rights, liberties, and satisfactions of the civilian' (A 130).

One of the civilian 'satisfactions' which is lost is the capacity to be
taken as the person one claims to be. For Goffman, this is significant
because one of his key ideas is that human interaction has a promissory

character. In *The Presentation of Self in Everyday Life*, he notes that 'during the period in which the individual is in the immediate presence of the others, few events may occur which directly provide the others with the conclusive information they will need if they are to direct wisely their own activity' (PS 13). There are, though, always elements which point towards the behaviour and attitudes of the person beyond the immediate encounter. These tokens are not strict scientific evidence of a certain character or personality type. Rather, they are more or less conventional signs of the individual's reliability. As Goffman implies, these signs are analogous to paper currency: 'others are likely to find that they must accept the individual on faith, offering him a just return while he is present before them in exchange for something whose true value will not be established until after he has left their presence' (PS 14). Self-presentation is a promissory note: the job candidate, for example, who dresses neatly, sits attentively, and speaks politely is offering a series of privileged signs which conventionally guarantee his future behaviour as a model employee. Furthermore, like the special paper, watermark and metal strip in a *bona fide* banknote, there are certain signs – instances of 'involuntary expressive behaviour' (PS 18) – which are regarded as insurance against counterfeit signs. The employer who, for example, is aware that the candidate may consciously adopt a responsible demeanour, scrutinises the interviewee for the supposed tell-tale indications of body language. Of course, even these privileged tokens may be faked. The candidate can learn to consciously provide such 'involuntary expressive behaviour' in order to satisfy the potential employer's expectations.

When Goffman extends his analysis to 'mental illness,' this capacity to counterfeit 'authentic' behaviour is revealed to be part of the patient's strategy for coping with an institutional environment. In most normal situations, one either has a large ability to sustain one's self conception, or to distance oneself from a threatening environment. At home and amongst friends, we may display ourselves to our best advantage. We are dressed, decorated, 'made-up,' so that others may have the privilege of confirming that we are just who we say we are. A mental hospital, however, is a total institution in which there is no refuge from such experiences. The patient is without control over her self-image, and lacks a refuge in which she may refresh her own self.

The mental hospital – and therapeutic practices such as group therapy – involve, notes Goffman, a sustained assault on the patient's self-presentations until (finally) the patient sincerely accepts his diagnosis. The institution has 'to show the ways in which the patient is "sick" [...]; and this is done by extracting from his whole life course a list of those incidents that have or might have had "symptomatic" significance' (A 144); the ultimate intention is that 'the patient must "insightfully" come to take, or affect to take, the hospital's view of himself' (A 143). However, a problem emerges precisely because of this demand for authentic acceptance from the patient that he 'has a problem.' In ordinary circumstances, self-presentations may be redeemed by spontaneous and uncoerced behaviours. However, in an institutional context, self-presentation is constantly adjusted toward institutional surveillance. It's as if one inhabits an economy where banknotes can only be exchanged for more banknotes; every action becomes a promissory note for an authentic selfhood which can never be reliably observed under the prevailing conditions. Goffman therefore implies that institutional 'diagnosis' and 'cure' may simply be a matter of the patient's ability to effectively 'pass-off' as first accepting his diagnosis, then insightfully working with the doctors towards recovery. The constant criticism and demands for reform teach the patient that 'a defensible picture of self can be seen as something outside oneself that can be constructed, lost, and rebuilt, all with great speed and some equanimity' (A 151).

Goffman further argues that, since patients have learned not to overtly resist their diagnostic label, they turn to surreptitious expressions of defiance. In a non-psychiatric institution, there are a variety of methods by which inmates can distance themselves from the regime: 'insolence, silence, *sotto voce* remarks, uncooperativeness, malicious destruction of interior decorations, and so forth' (A 269). In a psychiatric context, however, these are likely to be regarded as symptoms of 'mental illness,' and, therefore, as further evidence that the patient has been justly institutionalised:

From the patient's point of view, to decline to exchange a word with the staff or with his fellow patients may be ample evidence of rejecting the institution's view of what and who he is; yet higher management may construe this alienative expression as just the sort of symptomatology the institution was established to deal with. (A 268)

Mutism, 'dirty' protests, refusal to dress or work, and so on, are likely to be taken as neurotic or psychotic behaviour.

As well as interpreting the impact upon selfhood of institutional experience, Goffman also discusses how certain acts come to be taken as expressions of 'mental illness.' In his essay 'The Insanity of Place' (1969), he notes that

a social deviation can hardly be reckoned apart from the relationships and organizational memberships of the offender and offended, since there is hardly a social act that in itself is not appropriate or at least excusable in some social context. The delusions of a private can be the rights of a general; the obscene invitations of a man to a strange girl can be the spicy endearments of a husband to his wife; the wariness of a paranoid is the warranted practice of thousands of undercover agents. (IPl 368–69)

The sociological analysis of the 'madman's' deviance is deepened by Thomas Scheff's *Being Mentally Ill* (1966), which puts forward an extended argument on the way social processes may construct a confirmed mental patient. Scheff draws attention to the various ways in which rule-breaking, or 'deviance,' may lead to such labels as 'ill-mannered, ignorant, sinful, criminal' (BMI 32). In these instances, the deviant individual breaks rules which are fairly well articulated: he defies (although perhaps unwittingly) standards of politeness, intelligence, morality, and legality. On the other hand, there exists, as Scheff points out, a whole world of rules which are so generally taken for granted that they are never articulated. The 'mentally ill' individual comes to the attention of his community because he breaks these left-over, residual rules in a display of 'residual deviance.' For example, there is no rule in the Bible, the lawbooks, schoolbooks, or etiquette guides that one *should not* conduct spoken conversations with individuals who are imaginary or physically absent; it is generally assumed that one should do so only 'internally,' or in certain recognised contexts (such as while praying, or rehearsing one's lines in a play). Whatever the 'cause' – bodily, circumstantial, psychological, or volitional – of such contextually inappropriate behaviour, the primary sociological fact is a display of residual deviance.

What fascinates Scheff is the way in which, through purely sociological (and largely involuntary) phenomena, residual deviance can become a habitual pattern of behaviour for a confirmed 'mentally ill' agent. Left to his own devices, notes Scheff (and here he echoes Goffman), the individual may terminate residually deviant behaviour, or find a context in which it is ignored, denied, or even valued (for example, as a 'nutty' professor). However, if the individual is faced with a diagnosis of 'mental illness,' and with consequent treatment, then he is put in a difficult and threatening position. In order to cope with this new social position, he is motivated to both amplify and stabilise his 'mentally ill' behaviour. This feedback loop occurs because of precisely the same normative phenomena which made deviance possible in the first place. The deviant individual is now someone whose deviance is normal; he is a typecast actor, who is expected to be 'mad,' and who expects himself to be 'mad,' and who may even find utilitarian benefits in accepting and cultivating his role. This is not necessarily to say that the agent is intentionally malingering; rather, 'mentally ill' behaviour is a *savoir faire* which is acquired as one enters the role. It is as pointless to blame the individual for his behaviour, one might say, as to condemn an immigrant for picking up the accent of his new country.

Scheff and Goffman provide two complementary sociological accounts of 'mental illness' which both challenge the assumed reality of the condition. They argue against the assumption that the condition is 'in' the individual, and must be 'treated' by modifying the 'afflicted' person. For Goffman, 'mental illness' is a process of labelling and institutionalisation which erodes the patient's capacity for uncalculated self-presentation. The mental patient wants to cry out loud 'I'm not crazy, I tell you!', but (quite rationally) recognises that this is imprudent. He therefore forges (in both senses) a counterfeit personality to armour his own conviction that he is both sane and normal – a belief which emerges in seemingly insane acts of defiance. In Scheff's analysis, a competing, but equally sceptical account is presented: instead of losing spontaneity in an institutional context and engaging in deviant acts of resistance, the 'mentally ill' person internalises the role that is pointed out by those around him. Scheff's patient instead cries out wholeheartedly 'I *am* mad, I tell you!', so beginning a potentially lengthy and perhaps perversely rewarding career in residual deviance.

Thomas Szasz

Thomas Szasz was born in Hungary in 1920, but relocated to the United States when he was eighteen. He studied first physics, and then medicine, before training at the Chicago Institute of Psychoanalysis. Although he refuses the label 'anti-psychiatrist,' Szasz is still active as a prolific critic of the tendency to turn human woes and misbehaviour into instances of 'mental illness.' His reputation was assured when, in 1961, he published *The Myth of Mental Illness*, in which he sought to demonstrate that the very notion of 'mental illness' is a mistaken metaphor. Szasz's thesis was instantly controversial, but also extremely influential. Clearly, Szasz does not deny that people approach their doctors with all kinds of unusual behaviour and attitudes; the myth, argues Szasz, is that such individuals should be classified as 'mentally ill.'

There is a clear conceptual affinity between Szasz's work and that of Goffman and Scheff. Szasz – in his early work, at least – contends that 'mental illness' arises in the presentation of (putatively) hard-to-counterfeit signs that someone is unable to care for him- or herself. By this means, the patient acquires, howsoever unconsciously, some advantage from their status as a 'sick' person. This argument is spelled out in detail in *The Myth of Mental Illness* where, drawing upon the theories of the American philosopher, George Herbert Mead, Szasz advances a theory of 'mental illness' using a 'game-playing' model of human behaviour. 'Mental illness' is the game-playing tactic adopted, argues Szasz, by those who are dissatisfied with the rules of the game in which they are a player. It is 'a culturally shared *folie*' (MMI 234) in which 'persons impersonate the roles of helplessness, hopelessness, weakness, and often of bodily illness – when, in fact, their actual roles pertain to frustrations, unhappinesses, and perplexities due to interpersonal, social, and ethical conflicts' (MMI 233). Such impersonation, Szasz perceives, is a very ordinary phenomenon with no particular psychiatric significance. He cites the example of a Depression-era veteran of World War One who pretends to sell apples but is in fact begging. The indigent's pretence allows him to beg without drawing attention to the unpleasant truth that a man who has served his country is reduced to such penury that he must ask for money. In such circumstances, the easiest way to achieve his goal is to play a role with which those around him collude. Such behaviour embodies Szasz's early, 'transactional' model of 'mental illness' in which the 'mentally ill' take on a sick role in order to acquire certain advantages. They cannot openly reach for these aims because of social prohibitions or personal unwillingness. Just as the apple seller solves the problem of obtaining money without appearing to beg, so the 'mentally ill' patient indirectly obtains a goal which she is unable (in a broad sense) to directly communicate. This inability to tell the truth about one's needs arises because, notes Szasz, *'to be able to be truthful one must be more or less grown up and personally secure, and one must live in a social situation which encourages, or at least permits, truthfulness'* (MMI 228).

Szasz's favoured example of psychiatric impersonation is hysteria, in which, he argues, the patient imitates physical weakness in order to secure some unacknowledged goal. In a book of psychiatric aphorisms, *The Second Sin* (1973), Szasz also expands this model to other realms of 'mental illness:'

> The so-called mental patient makes statements and presents dramatizations which do not assert any facts, but rather command the onlooker to some sort of action. [...]. The agitated self-accusatory 'depressed' person commands: 'You must dominate me: hate me, punish me, etc.' (SS 91)

Szasz suggests further roles which are projected by other 'mental illnesses.' Depression is 'a caricature of contrition;' obsessive-compulsion, 'a caricature of conscientiousness;' and paranoia, 'a caricature of concern with betrayal, danger, and protection' (SS 95). The motive for such self-presentations, of course, may vary enormously. The phobic, for example, may transform an 'empty life [...] into a life full of interesting dangers, threats, and terrors. This solves the patient's problem of what to do with his life' (SS 94). An hysteric may mimic physical illness in order to convey the message 'I can't get up and go out and do things with or for you' (SS 93). Unlike, for example, 'a small boy playing fireman' (SS 52), these impersonations are not socially recognised as such; indeed, if 'persons stubbornly cling to and aggressively proclaim publicly unsupported role definitions, they are called psychotic' (SS 52).

A further strand of Szasz's argument is concerned with the normative basis of psychiatric diagnosis. Indeed, as Szasz's work develops, this libertarian motif becomes the most pervasive of his criticisms. What concerns Szasz is the way in which medical science investigates the

causes of so-called 'mental illness' without first considering the normative basis of diagnosis. What right does the psychiatrist have to impose
his own standards of normality and deviance on the patient? Or why,
even if the patient demands that he be regarded as 'mentally ill,' should
the psychiatrist accept this evaluation? Szasz sums up his position:

Psychiatric diagnoses are stigmatising labels phrased to resemble medical diagnoses and applied to persons whose behaviour annoys or offends others. Those
who suffer from and complain of their own behaviour are usually classified as
'neurotic:' those whose behaviour makes others suffer, and about whom others
complain, are usually classified as 'psychotic.' (SS 16)

The whole process of psychiatric diagnosis and treatment, for Szasz,
flows from this fundamental, but unspoken belief, that (as another aph-
orism puts it), 'if the patient were well, he would live as we do, not as he
does' (SS 92). Psychiatry is too frequently the search for a means – rhetorical, pharmacological, microsurgical – by which the patient can be
compelled to conform to some socially current ideal of behaviour.

Szasz's model of illness is convincing but, if anything, it is too narrow:
he does not recognise how widely the normative model applies. For
Szasz, plausibly enough, the central idea of disease is an easily identifia-
ble physical illness. He argues in *Insanity: The Idea and its Consequences*
(1987) that 'the sorts of items that comprise the core concept of disease'
are 'abnormal bodies, organs, tissues, cells, and physiological processes'
(I 12). He refers to these conditions as '*bodily diseases* or *real diseases* or
simply *diseases*' (I 12). Szasz feels secure in the objectivity of this category; he claims that the 'decisive initial step I take is to *define illness as the
pathologist defines it – as a structural or functional abnormality of cells, tissues,
organs, or bodies*' (I 12). Yet, when Szasz later refers to this core concept as
a matter of 'deviations from biological norms,' (I 19) then it is clear that
something has gone awry – for how can biology be normative, unless,
of course, one is really referring to norms of physical well-being? In his
essay 'The Insanity of Place,' Goffman is beset by a similar difficulty. He
considers the relations between 'mental illness' and issues of self-
definition. He emphasises that 'medical symptoms and mental
symptoms, so-called, are radically different things' (IP 385). Like Szasz,
he over-optimistically affirms that 'signs and symptoms of a *medical* disorder presumably refer to underlying pathologies in the individual

organism, and these constitute deviations from biological norms maintained by the homeostatic functioning of the human machine' (IP 362). Deviations from cultural expectations of ill-health, Goffman believes, can fundamentally be traced to disorders in the balance of bodily processes.

The distinction between medical and mental symptoms is facile, however. As Peter Sedgwick has argued in *Psycho Politics* (1982),

> critical theory in psychiatry has tended to postulate a fundamental separation between 'mental illnesses' and the general run of human ailments: the former are the expression of social norms, the latter proceed from ascertainable bodily states which have an 'objective existence within the individual.' (PP 28)

But, '*All sickness is essentially deviancy.* That is to say, no attribution of sickness to any being can be made without the expectation of some alternative state of affairs which is considered more desirable' (PP 32). Without human projections, there is no substance to terms such as 'health' or 'illness:' 'the fracture of a septuagenarian's femur has, within the world of nature, no more significance than the snapping of an autumn leaf from its twig' (PP 30). Although medical science is, of course, concerned with objective biological realities, the motive for its investigation, and its basis for the delineation of medical phenomena, is our human dissatisfaction with our being: a species without ill health might take an idle amusement in examining the workings of the body; but we are fragile beings, whose health is frequently threatened.

To be fair to Szasz and Goffman, though, physical health is probably a far less variable and culturally contingent notion than 'mental health.' The normative basis to physical diagnosis is largely taken for granted: to live long and actively, to have the full use of all our senses, to be free of pain – these and other ideals of health are widely and generally accepted. However, in illness of the 'soul,' as we might expect, normative ideals are far more obvious. Goffman and Szasz are therefore on firmer ground when they expose the normativity of 'mental health.' Indeed, as others have noted, the deviance in 'madness' varies over time even in Western culture. The French historian and philosopher Michel Foucault argues, for example, that the nature of such deviance was very different in seventeenth-century France. In *Madness and Civilization* (1967), the

English language edition of *Folie et déraison* (1961), Foucault traces asylums to great seventeenth-century European confinements of beggars, impoverished students, and wastrels. These also sweep up the 'mad:'

In the classical age, for the first time, madness was perceived through a condemnation of idleness and in a social immanence guaranteed by the community of labor. This community acquired an ethical power of segregation, which permitted it to eject, as into another world, all forms of social uselessness. (MCi 58)

Madness, argues Foucault, was then deviant because it was economically unproductive.

However, whatever the defects of the typical anti-psychiatric model of physical illness, we can surely accept the general thesis on the normativity of psychiatric diagnosis. Szasz, for example, lucidly points out that much psychoanalysis persuades another person to change his behaviour (or at least regard it as deviant) by a kind of rhetorical victory:

when a man has sexual relations with many women, psychoanalysts say he has a Don Juan complex which signifies latent homosexuality. But when a man has sexual relations with many men psychoanalysts do not say he has an Oscar Wilde complex which signifies latent heterosexuality. (SS 84)

Central to psychoanalysis is a 'vocabulary [...] rich in images and terms that demean and invalidate, and poor in those that dignify and validate' (SS 84). Alongside these rhetorical tactics, are the cruder instruments of medication and surgery, and the use of involuntary mental hospitalisation upon those who refuse them. Indeed, for Szasz, involuntary institutionalisation is merely a kind of imprisonment. His essay 'Involuntary Mental Hospitalization: A Crime Against Humanity' (1967) in *Ideology and Insanity* (1991), argues that the closest analogy to commitment is slavery. In both cases, a paternalistic, yet exploitative class of people systematically deprive another, 'lower' group of their autonomy – and should the latter group refuse to consent to their imprisonment, it is because their inferiority (their 'race' or their 'illness') means they cannot recognise the necessity of this degradation.

Szasz's attempts to render 'mental illness' intelligible, to expose the 'unconscious mind' as a rhetorical fiction, and to reveal the hidden normative basis of diagnosis might make him appear to be a paradigm anti-psychiatrist – a figure as typical, perhaps, as Laing himself. Yet, in a 1976 article, 'Anti-Psychiatry: The Paradigm of the Plundered Mind,' Szasz spells out his perceived distance from the anti-psychiatrists (principally Laing and his occasional collaborator, David Cooper): 'I reject the term "anti-psychiatry,"' he declares, 'because it is imprecise, misleading, and cheaply self-aggrandising' (AP 3). Much of this opposition arises from Szasz's political stance. He contends (rightly or wrongly) that the therapeutic communities with which Laing is associated are state-funded, thereby replacing 'the coercion of the mental patient by the psychiatrist on behalf of the citizen, with the coercion of the taxpayer by the government on behalf of the mental patient' (AP 4). It is hard, though, to take seriously Szasz's outrage at either the redistribution of wealth, or the commonplace that, in a representative democracy, the taxpayer may indeed lack a direct vote on the precise allocation of revenues.

Szasz's other argument is more interesting: 'anti-psychiatrists have borrowed the model of exploitation – of colonialism, foreign invasion, and plunder – from the Old Left' (AP 13). What is plundered, he contends, is a fictional notion of

an authentic or true self, which is conceived of, in the Rousseauesque tradition, as also a universal human possession or potentiality, and it too is achieved without personal effort; and insanity results from damage to or loss of this treasured possession to which everyone has a sort of 'political right.' (AP 14)

This is partly accurate: Laing certainly argues that the 'divided self' of the schizophrenic is colonised and damaged. However, as we shall see, the Rousseauesque ideal is a symptom of this colonisation. It is only when the self has retreated into a purely interior life, that spontaneity is confused with the effortlessness of thought and imagination. It is certainly not accurate to suggest that, for Laing, 'what the schizophrenic has more of than other people is "authenticity"' (AP 6); what the schizophrenic, or, more fundamentally, the 'schizoid' has is *less* capacity for feeling that they are what they do and say and feel. Laing does, at one point, argue that schizophrenics have deeper insight into the contingency of the social constructions which shape experience – but this anthropologically inspired idea is far removed from Szasz's existential notion of 'an authentic or true self.'

David Cooper

David Cooper was born in Cape Town, South Africa in 1931. After studying at the University of Cape Town, Cooper appears to have undergone an unusual postgraduate training. According to Laing, 'David [Cooper] was a trained Communist revolutionary, and was a member of the South African Communist Party. He was sent to Poland and Russia and China to be trained as a professional revolutionary' (MTBN 194). Cooper began working as a psychiatrist because when he relocated to London he was afraid to return to South Africa as a 'marked man' (MTBN 195). Cooper published various works critical of psychiatry, and collaborated with Laing on *Reason and Violence* (1964). He continued publishing throughout the 1970s, and lived in various locations around the world. He died in 1986 in Paris.

In *Psychiatry and Anti-Psychiatry* (1967), Cooper refers to research by Gregory Bateson and Don Jackson which analyses a particular communicative dilemma – that of the 'double bind.' Cooper quotes Bateson and Jackson on contexts where 'the individual is caught in a situation in which the other person in the relationship is expressing two orders of message and one of these denies the other' (PAP 57). The individual, however, 'is unable to comment on the messages being expressed to correct his discrimination of what order of message to respond to, i.e., he cannot make a metacommunicative statement' (PAP 57). This might seem a trivial problem: but a double bind can be a frustrating situation even outside of intense family relationships. A mundane example may prove useful. Certain everyday situations, which may even appear to demand honesty, in fact discourage it. A job interview is a human interaction in which the candidate attempts to persuade the potential employer of her suitability for the post. Consider a job interview in which a panel member asks the candidate, 'what are your weaknesses?'. A full and pertinent answer to this question would require the candidate to dissuade the employer from making an offer. However, to refuse to answer the question would also be dissuasive since it implies that the candidate would make a disobedient employee. An obvious, straightforward lie ('I have no weaknesses') is equally prejudicial – a good employee, after all, is an honest employee; and, indeed, even if it were true that the candidate had no weaknesses, she cannot risk appearing arrogant enough to say so. One could risk explicitly stating this dilemma; but few interview panels would tolerate such presumption, and would no doubt be frustrated by the candidate's unwillingness to supply 'just an honest answer.'

Without such a 'metacommunicative' statement, however, an attempt to respond in this context to the question 'what are your weaknesses?' is likely to involve behaviour which, amplified and continued, might receive the label 'mentally ill.' The candidate will attempt some non-verbal communication of honesty: a pensive expression, an apparent reluctance, a show of embarrassment and inferiority. This may then be melded with a verbal communication that is, nonetheless, a failure in honesty. She can supply a trivial or irrelevant weakness, or a personal failing that is really a boon to the employer ('working too hard,' for example). She may present a weakness and then assert her way of elimi-nating the weakness; such a weakness, of course, is no longer an actual weakness – it is a potential weakness, which has been eliminated. Such communication could be regarded as displaying a degree of 'thought disorder' in the answer.

'Mental illness,' Cooper suggests, may arise when an individual lives twenty-four hours a day, seven days a week, in a family where this com-municative pattern is the norm. Cooper analyses an extended case study, that of 'Eric,' a university student diagnosed as schizophrenic. Eric's 'ill-ness,' Cooper argues, really indicates 'that Eric had never carried out a single independent act in his life' (PAP 73). Much of Eric's seeming madness is an attempt to act autonomously, but this self-assertion is fundamentally limited by a double bind because

his parents persistently invited him to assert himself independently in all sorts of ways while remaining impervious to his own attempt to do so. If he were to take up his parents' invitation he would fall into a trap because he would then once again be merely following their direction. (PAP 73–74)

Eric is caught in multiple double-binds which have the general form of the (self-defeating) command 'Be autonomous!'. By telling Eric to do what he wants to do anyway, his parents alchemically convert his free actions into proof of his obedience. Their apparently supportive desire for his freedom is, in fact, a way of surreptitiously requiring his continued submission. Eric's bizarre return home from university is a way of responding to this double bind; it is

a negativity, a non-act or the reverse side of a positive act, by which he set the stage for his first big autonomous action. He came home from the university to which he had been sent *in order to go to the university.* As soon as he arrived home he wanted to return – but return by his own choice. (PAP 73)

How, Cooper asks, can we expect anything other from such situations than the seeming malfunction of thought and feeling in 'psychotic confusion, thought disorder, catatonia, and so on'? (PAP 38).

Cooper does not believe standard therapeutic methods are at all adequate to dealing with such cases. A patient is typically isolated from the very social context which requires analysis. Eric's actions, for example, were unintelligible if his activities were abstracted from his relations to his other family members. In context, though, his seemingly disordered activities and thoughts expressed his need for autonomy. Indeed, it is hard to see how a conventional institutional setting could help patients like Eric recover, given that they usually require the patient to be passive until 'the *mise en scène* of the psychiatrist who [...] cures the rot' (PAP 41). How can a 'patient' regain her autonomy when he is coercively abstracted from society, browbeaten into passivity, and encouraged to regard his own actions as the alien intrusions of his disease?

Cooper also mischievously exploits the rhetoric of 'mental illness.' Since many disease symptoms indicate healing processes, might not this be extended to the 'symptomatology' of a 'diseased' mind? He speculates that the process of disintegration in 'mental illness' might be the most vital of the patient's actions. With this thought, Cooper advances one of the most controversial of anti-psychiatric doctrines: that 'psychotic experience may, with correct guidance, lead to a more advanced human state' (PAP 93). Cooper contrasts our modern society with 'primitive' shamanistic societies which have socially validated contexts for experiences of personal disintegration and renewal. Sometimes, Cooper states, 'one needs to be allowed to go to pieces and one needs to be helped to come together again' (PAP 92). There are, he believes, many different forms this process may take – he includes psychotic episodes, drug use, and aesthetic experience. They are all branches of potential or actual 'discipline[s] for disintegration' (PAP 95). How, though, may this process come to fruition when, behind the apparent innocence of a 'talking cure' there may lurk a variety of sanctions? Even a patient who is not institutionalised may perceive that his continued liberty requires that he respond 'sanely' to his interlocutor. Cooper refers to the French writer Antonin Artaud's dialogues with his psychiatrist, and notes that 'at the final critical moment of the dialogue the rub was always this: "If you speak of bewitchment again, M. Artaud, you shall have 65 electro-shocks"' (PAP 47).

Cooper's apology for madness may indeed seem controversial, but it is moderate when compared to some of his later utterances. In *The Grammar of Living* (1974), he refers to a peculiar practice known as 'bed therapy' which may, he tells us, be 'the only right move at a certain critical junction according to a coincidence of needs of both people concerned' (GL 115). Given that sex is liberation, implies Cooper, then it need not be inappropriate for a 'therapist' to have sex with a 'patient.' Look, after all, at the 'pathetic non-orgasmic faces of the bourgeois puppet "leaders," the Hitlers, Nixons, etc.' (GL 52). In *The Language of Madness* (1978), Cooper's peculiar sexual statements continue. He even asserts that 'the menopausal changes in women are socially conditioned and should be socially-politically reversible' (LM 68). Cooper (incredibly enough) argues that the cessation of ovulation is directly an effect of a particular economic system: menopause is 'our human invention in terms of reproductivity of man-power for the system of property' (LM 68).

In the same book, Cooper recalls that 'in the early 1962, in the course of various polemics in England, I produced finally the wretched and infinitely distorted term "anti-psychiatry"' (LM 126). Earlier, he notes in *The Grammar of Living* that 'a mythical and mystique-full web [...] was later generated around this apparently simple hyphenated word' (GL 54). If 'anti-psychiatry' became an 'onerous label' (GL 54), then Cooper is hardly blameless. His latter propensity for messianic statements with only the slightest connection to evidence or logical thought helped to bring into discredit the movement he named. And, of course, Cooper's association with Laing also brought the latter's usually far more moderate ideas into disrepute.

Literary anti-psychiatry

Creative literature has often taken an interest in the 'mad.' Writers have frequently tackled 'mental illness,' often with the aim of displaying its inner intelligibility. A significant example from the 'anti-psychiatric' period is Valeriy Tarsis' *Ward 7*, which was published in the United Kingdom in 1965. Tarsis, a citizen of the Soviet Union, was institutionalised for several months after the publication in 1962 of *The Bluebottle*, a novel critical of the Kruschev-era USSR. *Ward 7* is not a great work of literature: it is an autobiographical novella with frequent, and ultimately tedious, reflections on 'the herd,' 'the apes,' and 'the serfs' who interfere with the glorious destiny of Russian artists. Even more ludicrous is its nostalgia for a 'primitive community' in which men are 'conducted like a choir by some elder who had neither weapons nor guards but was nevertheless respected and implicitly obeyed' (W7 86).

Nonetheless, the novel has a value beyond mere reportage. A dialogue, for example, is conducted between two characters: the Russian psychiatrist Professor Nezhevsky and the French psychiatrist René Gillard. Despite his work within the Soviet system, Nezhevsky is quite aware of the political meaning of his diagnoses. The narrator informs us that Nezhevsky 'dismissed the current notion of "mental illness" – if only because no one could give a definition of mental health, so that there was no firm principle by which to define or classify pathological phenomena' (W7 119–20). Indeed, not only are standards of 'mental health' normative, there is, argues Nezhevsky, a sense in which 'mental illness' is an intelligible response to Soviet society: 'You realise that almost the whole country lived in panic terror for decades? You could safely diagnose every Russian as suffering from persecution mania' (W7 120). Furthermore, continues Nezhevsky, 'our whole national way of life is such as to aggravate the state of depression – everlasting want, anxiety to make ends meet, privations, insecurity' (W7 121). The narrator also pursues this line of argument: 'failed suicides' are

classified as lunatics because it was assumed (by doctors and politicians, writers and ideologists) that anyone dissatisfied with the socialist paradise must be a lunatic, and the doctors had conveniently produced the theory that only a lunatic was capable of making an attempt on his own life. (W7 22)

Although *Ward 7* is intended as a critique of Soviet systems (and, indeed, naively idealises the West), its presentation of psychiatrically mediated political repression asks universal questions. Might not the West also have political reasons for classifying as insane those who feel persecuted, depressed, or suicidal? To diagnose these as 'mental health' issues in the West is also to make a hidden normative assessment, and perhaps to imply that those who feel this way can have no intelligible reasons for their behaviour.

Ken Kesey's novel, *One Flew Over the Cuckoo's Nest* (1962) develops a similar argument in its depiction of a 'mental health' institution in the USA. The story tells of Macmurphy, a convict who fakes madness in order to be transferred from a penitentiary to a mental hospital, where, he believes, he will find more comfortable conditions. He encourages the patients at the hospital, many of whom are voluntarily committed, to rebel against the dehumanising regime and its functionary, Nurse Ratched. Macmurphy eventually sexually assaults Nurse Ratched when she drives one of the patients to suicide. He is then referred for lobotomy, and returns to the ward brain-damaged and speechless. He is compassionately smothered to death by the story's Native American narrator, 'Chief Bromden,' who then makes his escape from the hospital.

The novel presents psychiatric institutions as largely a mechanism for the control of deviance. The clearest example of this is a character who is homosexual but who has committed himself in order to be 'cured' of his desires. In no sense, though, is this character 'mentally ill:' he is simply someone who offends the socially-current and state-sanctioned sexual mores current in the United States of America during the late 1950s. Like *Ward 7*, Kesey's novel therefore exposes the political misuse of psychiatry. This thesis is emphasised and elaborated throughout the novel by a recurrent comparison of the mental hospital with a miniature totalitarian state. The residents are encouraged to record information about other patients for the scrutiny of Nurse Ratched, just as, for example, citizens are encouraged to inform on friends and neighbours in a police state. Furthermore, Macmurphy frequently compares the ward with his experiences in a PoW camp during the Korean War. Group therapy is presented through Macmurphy as a show trial in which a deviant individual is subject to a degrading interrogation, and which concludes with an act of ritual submission to the therapeutic 'regime.' Indeed, it seems likely that reports of 'brain-washing' in the Korean war were a significant inspiration for US anti-psychiatry. An article by Robert J. Lifton gives the flavour of this 'peculiar brand of soul surgery' (TR 173) employed by the Chinese state on both Western civilians and prisoners-of-war. Lifton describes the process by which the authorities attempted to change the thoughts of those they had imprisoned. The inmate is interrogated with a constant demand that he confess his crime; only the admission (sincere or not) of some wrongdoing is sufficient to bring about leniency. This procedure culminates in a stage in which the prisoner

must constantly 'analyze' his alleged deficiencies, his 'thought problems,' and his 'resistances.' 'Depth interpretations' are available for all varieties of nonconformity. Everything is reducible to the 'insights' of the Marxist doctrine: he 'works through' every barrier to 'reform.' (TR 191)

With its emphasis on confession and soul-searching reform, this process is all too similar to institutional group therapy. For example, in group meetings, 'each prisoner must examine his own "reactionary" tendencies, and then search out the causes for these in his early life' (TR 186) while those around him are 'on the lookout for any tendency to resist full emotional participation' (TR 186).

Although the film version in 1975 of *One Flew over the Cuckoo's Nest* presents Macmurphy as the focus of the story, the novel is concerned more with the redemption of its narrator, Chief Bromden, through Macmurphy's self-sacrifice. A great deal of extra anti-psychiatric perspective is presented in Bromden's narrative. He experiences delusions and hallucinations that the ward is an enormous machine which implants electronic control mechanisms in its patients. Although delusional, Bromden's experience is insightful. The ward largely works by encouraging the deviant individuals to imagine themselves as malfunctioning mechanisms. Once this psychiatric explanation is 'implanted,' the patients unthinkingly acquiesce to the institute's attempts to restore normal 'functioning.' This same process is described in episodes from other literary works of the period. Although neither *Catch-22* (1961) by Joseph Heller, nor *Slaughterhouse-Five* (1969) by Kurt Vonnegut, have a sustained anti-psychiatric agenda, both books ridicule psychoanalytic 'explanations' which are essentially normative injunctions. In particular, they target an expectation that war should be a normal experience – that anyone who finds war hateful, disturbing, or unbearable is suffering from a mental condition. In *Catch-22*, a psychiatrist, Major Sanderson, instructs the protagonist, Yossarian, that he is 'immature […] unable to adjust to the idea of war' because of 'deep-seated survival anxieties' (C22 313). In *Slaughterhouse-Five*, the central character, Billy Pilgrim, commits himself to an institution because of his distress at his wartime experiences in Europe. His psychiatrists, however, engage in a psycho-analytic search for the 'real reason' that Billy cannot adjust to war: '[They] didn't think it had anything to do with the war. They were sure Billy was going to pieces because his father had thrown him into the deep end of the Y.M.C.A. swimming pool when he was a little boy, and had then taken him to the rim of the Grand Canyon' (S5 72). They resemble Major Sanderson in *Catch-22* when Yossarian refuses the offer of a cigarette on the grounds of having just finished one. Sanderson chuckles, and remarks, 'That's a very ingenious explanation. But I suppose we'll soon discover the true reason' (C22 305).

Conclusion

'Anti-psychiatry,' even in just its English-speaking form, was a varied enterprise. Goffman revealed the effects upon patients of their institu-tionalisation in order to enquire whether this might better explain their 'symptoms' than the notion of 'mental illness.' Scheff also discussed sociologically the career path of the madman, and asked how far psychiatric diagnosis and treatment merely solidify an initial episode of deviance. Szasz unravelled philosophically the notion of 'mental illness' while also analysing the benefits that might accrue to someone cast in the 'sick role.' Cooper developed a theory of distorted communication within the family unit, and even argued that psychotic experience may potentially be beneficial to those who had been driven to 'madness.' Through fictional writing, the likes of Kesey explored both the totalitar-ian environment of the mental hospital, and the potential figurative truth of madness.

The anti-psychiatrists may have had a naive conception of the objectivity of physical illness. However, they all argued against the idea that 'mental illness' was a self-evident datum, a condition located in the individual that could immediately be scientifically categorised and analysed. Anti-psychiatrists perceived that attributions of 'mental illness' are essentially normative. To be 'mentally ill' is to deviate from expected standards of thought, action, and emotion. Paranoia, obsessive compulsion, and depression, for example, do not exist as things in themselves; rather, these modes of human being deviate from norms of rational concern, autonomy, and personal fulfilment, and so are categorised as a particular kind of deviance – as disease of the soul or mind. In this way, 'mental illness' is a social construction. Furthermore, such attributions show far more cultural variability than physical illness (where the 'constructedness' is harder to discern). What is 'madness' in one time or place is mental well-being in another, whereas attributions of physical illness tend to be far more stable and constant across cultures. With this analysis, psychiatric diagnosis and treatment was immediately exposed to a criticism based on civil liberties. As soon as the normative construction of psychiatric diagnosis was articulated, the question immediately arose as to whether these norms and expectations contradicted the rights and freedoms of the individual. What right does the state or the medical profession have to eliminate the 'residual deviance' or suicidal thoughts or other 'anti-social' expressions of the 'mentally ill'?

One of the primary deviations of the 'mentally ill' is the seeming unintelligibility of their behaviour: they seem to have 'lost their minds,' and to engage in behaviour which has no sense or purpose. Anti-psychiatrists therefore also sought to preserve the intelligibility and rationality of the 'mad.' Goffman showed, for example, how seemingly insane behaviour was a way of maintaining one's integrity within a total institution. Szasz and Scheff's typecast role-players are also acting in rational fashion. Even though they may not consciously feign illness to achieve their demands, there is at least a partial rationality in their strategic behaviour. The hysterical housewife, for example, rightly understands that only a feigned illness can successfully free her from the demands of conventional womanhood. Cooper follows a similar vein of thought. Why should his patient abruptly drop out of university? The answer is simple: he wants to verify that he himself can take this course of action, that he is not merely acquiescing in the demands of others. His behaviour, which seems irrational, is a reasonable attempt to cultivate his own freedom.

Although Laing was keenly aware of the social construction of 'mental illness,' and was also sensitive to rights of the 'mentally ill,' his work contributes most to the interpretation and understanding of such individuals. Throughout his career, he attempts to bridge the gap between the 'sane' and the 'mad' by transposing himself and his readers into the experience of those who are frequently regarded as the victims of unintelligible neurological and psychological processes.

Chapter Three

Work and Ideas

Laing's critical relation to mainstream psychiatry encompasses a number of different arguments and positions. The task of this chapter is to plausibly interpret and ground Laing's claims about the nature, meaning, and reality of 'mental illness.' I provide a broadly chronological exposition of his central ideas. Although there is not one single 'Laingean analysis,' codified and complete, there is a continuity and progression in Laing's arguments: different thoughts emerge, overlapping with preceding and succeeding concepts, creating not so much a chain of ideas as a weaving-together of various strands of thought. I concentrate on four motifs in Laing's work: the distinction between explaining a person's behaviour and understanding his or her words and actions; the anomalous and stigmatised experience of 'ontological insecurity' (and the 'divided self' that accompanies this condition); the role of interpersonal relations in Laing's analysis; and, finally, how Laing eventually regards our everyday 'sane' experience as a stifling social construction.

Explanation and understanding

A distinction central to Laing's thought, and one which is developed at length in *The Divided Self*, is that between *explanation* and *understanding*. When we explain some phenomenon we account for it by relating its existence to an initial set of conditions via a causal or statistical law. This kind of explanation is the paradigm in, say, physics and chemistry, and may also be employed in the social sciences. Yet, despite attempts to extend the reach of explanation, there remains, argues Laing, a kind of phenomenon which, though it may be explained, must primarily be understood. Laing illustrates the distinction very lucidly by applying it to a therapeutic meeting. He provides examples of how one might attempt to explain the behaviour of a patient:

If I am sitting opposite you and speaking to you, you may be trying (i) to assess any abnormalities in my speech, or (ii) to explain what I am saying in terms of how you imagine my brain cells to be metabolizing oxygen, or (iii) discover why, in terms of past history and socio-economic background, I should be saying these things at this time. (DS 33)

However, though one might explain what is being said in one of these ways, 'not one of the answers that you may or may not be able to supply to these questions will in itself supply you with a simple understanding of what I am getting at' (DS 33) – the sense of the words remains ungrasped by scientific description and explanation.

Laing therefore argues that explanatory models actually stand in the way of simply understanding what is being said and done by a patient. They encourage the therapist to examine the patient for signs and symptoms of disease in the way that one diagnoses a physical illness. Physical diagnosis consists in inspection of the patient for external signs (such as a rash), or in eliciting expressions of inner symptoms (such as feelings of malaise or pain). The problem with this mode of experiencing the psychiatric patient is that it automatically invokes explanation instead of understanding. As Laing once remarked in interview with Bob Mullan: 'what we needed was some sort of description which doesn't just describe what we see immediately in terms of signs and symptoms because a "sign" or a "symptom" of disease is actually a theory about the disease we are trying to describe' (MTBN 112).

Laing's distinction between explanation and understanding explicitly employs the work of Rudolf Bultmann, a twentieth-century German theologian. In 'The Problem of Hermeneutics,' an essay to which Laing refers in *The Divided Self,* Bultmann discusses the art of textual interpretation. No matter how foreign or baffling the text, the interpreter must always be guided by an initial intuition of a shared experience:

The presupposition of every comprehending interpretation is *a previous living relationship to the subject* [i.e. the subject-matter], which directly or indirectly finds expression in the text and which guides the direction of the enquiry. [...] In saying this we are also saying that every interpretation is necessarily sustained by a certain *prior understanding* of the subject which lies under discussion or in question. (PH 252)

For example I can only understand 'a novel because I know from my own life what [...] love and friendship, family and vocation, are' (PH

252). In any process of interpretation, I begin with this pre-understanding of what the text is about; this then functions as a guide which is revised as the text partly confirms, partly refuses, my initial understanding: 'It is of no value to eliminate the prior understanding: on the contrary, it is to be brought into our consciousness and critically tested in our understanding of the text' (PH 253–54).

Laing therefore employs a humanist paradigm for the psychotherapist. The therapist is no longer a scientist, inferring the causes which underlie the signs and symptoms exhibited by the patient – such hypotheses are a misuse of the patient's words. Rather, the therapist is an exegete, making sense of a puzzling and baffling text by drawing upon the possibilities of being which he shares with the patient:

> The personalities of doctor and psychotic, no less than the personalities of expositor and author, do not stand opposed to each other as two external facts that do not meet and cannot be compared. Like the expositor the therapist must have the plasticity to transpose himself into another strange and even alien view of the world. In this act, he draws on his own psychotic possibilities, without forgoing his sanity. (DS 34)

Laing's words even echo Bultmann's quotation of Wilhelm Dilthey, the nineteenth-century founder of modern hermeneutics, who declares that 'the individuality of the exegete and that of its author do not stand opposed to each other as two facts which cannot be compared' (PH 237–38). Of course, the exegesis of a psychotic may be difficult. One cannot assume that such an individual believes that 'he exists, in the world [...] as a permanent object in time and place, with others like himself' (DS 34). This, though, is a difference which Laing's own exegesis in *The Divided Self* will attempt to overcome.

Clearly enough, Laing's 'understanding' approach is inhospitable to neurological explanations. He is also, though, generally sceptical of psychoanalytic interpretation. This may seem surprising. Why should Laing, who is so keen on 'understanding,' refuse to 'interpret' psychoanalytically? Psychoanalytic interpretation involves scrutinising deviant actions and utterances for evidence of a repressed emotional conflict which renders them intelligible. The problem with 'interpretation' in this sense is that it too, like biochemical explanation, may be a way of not understanding the patient – the patient's communications are instantly transposed into signs and symptoms of a mental illness, the real meaning of which can only be revealed by a 'deep' interpretation. In his autobiography, *Wisdom, Madness, and Folly*, Laing recalls some Church of Scotland ministers who were discussing the responses to death amongst their parishioners. One told of an elderly man whose wife had just been buried: the widower turned to the minister and commented, 'You know, I've lived with that woman fifty years, and I never liked her' (WMF 136). This story, Laing recalls, 'evoked a ripple of understanding around his fellow ministers' (WMF 136). This understanding was at variance with Laing's own explanatory prejudices: 'It had never occurred to me that some sort of grief and mourning was not the usual response to bereavement. If it did not appear, then I automatically interpreted that as a manic defence' (WMF 136). Laing's model of grief following upon bereavement was intimately linked to the urge to interpret: by 'interpreting' the absence of grief as a defence, the explanatory rule was maintained, despite his contradictory understanding of the bereaved's words and actions.

There is a very standard complaint that Freudianism is pseudo-scientific precisely because the procedure of interpretation precludes any evidence which might disconfirm its hypotheses. This, though, is not Laing's point. He criticises Freudianism not because it fails to be a science, but because it even tries to be a science. This ambition inevitably impinges upon the understanding of what is being said by a patient. Karl Jaspers, the Continental philosopher and psychiatrist with whom Laing had planned to study, notes in the seventh edition of his *General Psychopathology* (1959), that 'the most radical mistakes spring from conclusions drawn as to the reality of what has been understood, whenever these conclusions have been based on the self-evidence of some one-sided understanding' (GP 357). To respond, for example, to bereavement with grief, or to respond with fortitude (or even indifference) may be equally intelligible. In either case, as Jaspers would insist, '*opposites are equally meaningful,*' – 'the exclusion of the opposite without any attempt to follow it up and understand it, means that we manipulate reality in favour of an "a priori" understanding that makes an arbitrary selection of the facts' (GP 357). Such is the case when, to use Laing's example, one interprets the absence of grief as a manic defence against that same emotion: the facts are manipulated into a rule (grief follows upon loss) which is neither an accurate understanding nor a valid scientific explanation.

Laing's wariness of the 'unconscious,' and his empathic method, are further illustrated by his case studies. In the case of 'Mrs R' in *The Divided Self*, Laing takes a typical mental illness, 'agoraphobia,' and attempts to understand what his patient's behaviour means without reference to Freudian hypotheses. Mrs R could be diagnosed as agoraphobic because she has 'a dread of being in the street' (DS 54). However, upon communicating further with Mrs R, Laing learns that 'her anxiety arose when she began to feel on her own in the street or elsewhere. She could *be* on her own, as long as she did not feel that she was really alone' (DS 54). Laing sketches Mrs R's current personal context. She is separated from her husband, and is now the mistress of a sculptor, but she still lives with her father, whom she cares for, just as earlier she cared for her dying mother. There is, notes Laing, an obvious psychoanalytic interpretation of this woman's anxiety in which she is regarded 'as unconsciously libidinally [i.e. sexually] bound to her father; with, consequently, unconscious guilt and unconscious need and/or fear of punishment' (DS 56). As supporting evidence, there is 'her failure to develop lasting libidinal relationships away from her father' and 'her decision to live with him' (DS 56). Her anxiety, then, is classically Freudian: it arises from her unconscious guilt at her unconscious incestuous fixation on her father. In such an interpretation, we have yet another victory for the Freudian 'laws' of psychic development in the individual.

Yet, argues Laing, this is just another way of refusing to encounter the patient. He sardonically counters, 'her fear of being alone is not a "defence" against incestuous phantasies. She had incestuous phantasies. *These phantasies were a defence against the dread of being alone*, as was her whole "fixation" on being a daughter' (DS 57). The woman's central experience was, in fact, of difficulty in experiencing her own existence: 'If she is not in the actual presence of another person who knows her, or if she cannot succeed in evoking this person's presence in his absence, her sense of her own identity drains away from her' (DS 56). Like 'Tinker Bell' in J.M. Barrie's play *Peter Pan*, this woman 'needs someone else to believe in her own existence' (DS 56). To understand the woman, one needs to understand this experience of threatened existence, a condition

which Laing designates 'ontological insecurity' (DS 39). Freudian interpretation, with its reference to 'phases of psychosexual development,
oral, anal, and genital' would simply obscure what was going on in this
woman's life – namely, that 'she could not be herself, by herself' (DS
58).

Laing's opposition to the 'unconscious mind,' though, is not
psychologically simplistic. He readily admits that his patient does not
understand herself very well – and in this sense she is 'unconscious' of
who she is. She will not gain any greater self-consciousness, though,
through a Freudian interpretation, for her own self-expressions would
be neither enriched nor clarified. Instead, such an analysis would insist
that her precarious sense of existence points to a repressed and deviant
psychosexual development. In this sense, Laing contends, Freudian
interpretation 'is in some measure an instrument of defence' (DS 25),
since it precisely obstructs an understanding of the patient's world by
invoking a pseudo-scientific theory of psychosexual development.

Ontological insecurity and the divided self

At the heart, then, of Laing's psychological exegesis in *The Divided Self* is
'ontological insecurity,' a genre of personality, as it were, which he
frequently detects in his patients (including Mrs R). This having 'life,
without feeling alive' (DS 40) requires considerable hermeneutic
'empathy;' yet, to Laing's credit, he provides a plausible account of this
condition. As the eminent British psychiatrist F.A. Jenner remarks, '[my
patients] came to me with a book called *The Divided Self*. They encouraged me to read it. They told me that if I wanted to understand them,
then here was a writer who had an inkling of what it was like to be mad'
(OL 91) – this was in contrast to the prevailing attitude that 'one of the
characterising definitions of psychosis was that it was impossible to
understand what the patient was saying' (OL 92).

Laing's notion of ontological insecurity revolves around the sufferer's
threatened and precarious sense of existence. The ontologically insecure
individual has difficulty, for example, in maintaining a sense of personal
continuity. He may be threatened by experiences such as sleep, where
self-consciousness is overpowered by natural forces and temporarily

dissolved: 'Going to sleep,' notes Laing, 'consists […] in a loss of one's awareness of one's being as well as that of the rest of the world' (DS 119); 'not to be conscious of oneself, therefore, may be equated with nonentity' (DS 119). The self is threatened not only by sleep. A further anxiety occurs in relation to what we now call 'flow' – experience in which, though consciousness is maintained, one's self-awareness disappears as one becomes absorbed in an experience:

sometimes the greatest reliance may be placed on the awareness of oneself in time. This is especially so when time is experienced as a succession of moments. The loss of a section of the linear temporal series of moments through inattention to one's time-self may be felt as a catastrophe. (DS 109)

Laing quotes a case-study which reveals precisely this anxiety of the ontologically insecure: 'I was so absorbed in looking at [the Ice Carnival] that I forgot what time it was and who and where I was. When I suddenly realized I hadn't been thinking about myself I was frightened to death. The unreality feeling came' (DS 109). If I am ontologically insecure, then, as Laing indicates, I substitute consciousness of self for my feeling of life. By knowing myself, by being an object of awareness, I am re-assured that I exist: I think of myself, therefore I am. Self-consciousness is an eternal vigilance which proves, through every instant, that 'I' exist. The ontologically insecure person is 'compulsively preoccupied with the sustained observation of his own mental and/or bodily processes' (DS 112).

The ontologically insecure person is threatened not just in temporal continuity. He may also feel only tenuously distinct from the world. Does he exist in his own right, or is he merely an outcrop or extension of a more substantial entity? To this kind of person, even the power of rational agreement may eliminate their sense of separate selfhood:

An argument occurred between two patients in the course of a session in an analytic group. Suddenly, one of the protagonists broke off the argument to say, 'I can't go on. You are arguing in order to have the pleasure of triumphing over me. At best you win an argument. At worst you lose an argument. *I am arguing in order to preserve my existence.*' (DS 43)

In thinking with the other, the ontologically insecure individual is swallowed up: their thoughts are not just the same (in agreement, 'qualitatively identical'); they are thinking the same thought (one single, 'numerically identical' thought). Indeed, for the ontologically insecure, any conscious life may be only precariously differentiated from that of other people. This is clear, for example, in the study of Peter, a young man who indulges in sadistic sexual fantasies in the toilets at his office:

> once [...] he emerged and encountered the very woman whom he had been raping in his mind. She was looking directly at him so that she seemed to look straight through him into his secret self and to see there what he had been doing to her. [...] He now could no longer believe with any assurance that he could conceal his actions and his thoughts from other people. (DS 124)

The ontologically insecure individual is in a dire position. He is unable to feel continuous and distinct, and he seeks endless re-assurance in compulsive self-consciousness (which provides a continual proof of his ongoing reality). This fragile introspective existence may be concealed by a split into a 'schizoid' or 'divided self' in which a 'false,' 'outer' self provides a buffer between self and others. Laing analyses this phenomenon in his case study of 'David,' a student who resembles 'an adolescent Kierkegaard played by Danny Kaye' (DS 70), and whose 'whole manner was entirely artificial' (DS 70). David's outer self is 'the part he regarded himself as having been playing most of his schooldays [...] that of a rather precocious schoolboy with a sharp wit, but somewhat cold' (DS 72). Using this self he can continue to be 'in entire conscious control of his expressions and actions, calculating with precision their effects on others' (DS 72). His spontaneous self exists behind this front: 'His ideal was *never to give himself away to others*' (DS 71). The advantage of his schizoid condition, David feels, is 'safety for the true self, isolation and hence freedom from others, self-sufficiency, and control' (DS 75).

Such schizoid existence is far from satisfactory. The divided self relates to the world via the known, outer self. For a spontaneous, living relationship with people and things, there is substituted the observation of the false self and the various entities to which it is related: 'direct and immediate transactions between the individual, the other, and the world, even in such basic respects as perceiving and acting, all come to be meaningless, futile, and false' (DS 80). This problem is particularly marked in personal relations. Instead of living immediately and spontaneously with others, the schizoid individual spectates upon dealings between the false self and others. Self and others in such instrumental dealings are not revealed as existing beings: 'There is a quasi-it-it interaction instead of an I-thou relationship' (DS 82). Inevitably, there results a failure in personal agency. The schizoid self merely spectates upon an alienated outer being, which seems hopelessly enmeshed in the chains of natural causality.

Indeed, so unsatisfactory is observation of 'life,' the inner self may even attempt to create imaginary objects of 'spontaneous' relationship. One of Laing's patients reveals this condition in his complaint that

he could never have intercourse with his wife but only with his own image of her. That is, his body had physical relations with her body, but his mental self, while this was going on, could only look on at what his body was doing and/or *imagine* himself having intercourse with his wife as an object of his imagination. (DS 86)

This peculiar condition, notes Laing, is but a whisker away from psychosis: 'This patient would have been psychotic, for instance, if, instead of saying that he never had intercourse with this wife "really," he had insisted that the woman with whom he had intercourse, was not his real wife' (DS 87). In this hypothetical instance, 'the individual expresses the "existential" truth about himself with the same matter-of-factness that we employ about facts that can be consensually validated in a shared world' (DS 87). These expressions, though meaningful, sound like sheer madness because of our own (philosophical) prejudices about truth. Our prejudice, Laing believes, is to consider as meaningful and (potentially) truthful only statements of logical equivalence, or verifiable explanations of the natural world. This bias blinds us, though, to the existential truth of remarks about 'reality' in which, for example, the schizoid may reveal his distance from immediate experience. For example, 'depersonalized patients' may 'speak of having murdered their selves' – 'such statements are usually called delusions, but if they are delusions, they are delusions which contain existential truth' (DS 49).

Of course, such statements are hard to understand because most of us are usually ontologically secure. We do not fear that we might wink out of existence, or dissolve into the world or other people, and we don't generally feel that our minds are distinct from our body. This is not the logic, though, of ontologically insecure experience. There, I may have difficulty believing that I exist continuously through time as an entity distinct from other people. I may feel that my real personality is a self-conscious mental self which lurks behind a false, bodily shell. This alienation from my body can lead to a sense of diminished agency: my outer self seems caught in a series of external causality with which my 'mind' cannot engage. My attempts to communicate my condition to others may then seem incomprehensible. In which case, I am likely to be further obliterated: others will treat me not as a person who can be understood, but as an object – a non-person – who may only be explained.

Understanding self and other

Despite the success of *The Divided Self*, the vocabulary of 'ontological insecurity' rarely appears throughout the rest of Laing's work. Instead, in the period immediately following *The Divided Self*, the emphasis moves towards understanding the schizoid retreat from embodied interaction. 'Ontological insecurity' can be re-interpreted according to this model. Most of us, most of the time, feel that we are bounded by our bodies. I live in my body, and deal with a world of other people and things. However, I could, in principle, have a larger, or non-existent, boundary to myself. I might, for example, regard others as puppets of my will, and believe that my breath animates the movement of the clouds. Alternatively, I could, as in the schizoid condition, have a much narrower personal boundary. I can withdraw from my body, and treat it as a thing external to myself, which moves according to its own mechanical laws. I can therefore choose to dwell solely in the realm of private images; I may even think of these as mine only when supplemented by self-conscious reflection. From this narrowing of experience derive many of the manifestations of ontological insecurity. If what is me is limited to self-conscious experience, then unthinking absorption into my life ('flow') will count as self-destruction. If I am not my body, then sleep is a temporary death; my body may continue during the night, but 'I' do not. Hunger and desire will press upon me like alien forces; they belong to my 'body,' so I do not experience them as spontaneous expressions of my self. If the thoughts of others enter my head, then I have, in a way, been possessed – for all that can be traced to me is the procession of thoughts, conceptions, and fantasies which parade through my private experience.

In the phase after *The Divided Self*, Laing sets himself to understand schizoid division as an intelligible response to interpersonal relations, rather than as a manifestation of ontological insecurity. What must be emphasised is that at least one idea in Laing's approach remains constant: the centrality of understanding as opposed to explanation. *Interpersonal Perception*, Laing's collaboration with Herbert Phillipson and Russell Lee, reminds the reader that the interpretative approach must be maintained in interpersonal analysis. There is no psychiatric validity in treating interpersonal experience in the explanatory mode, as if it were 'the direct consequence of physical behavioural impact (as when one billiard ball hits another)' (IP 13). Rather, 'experience in all cases entails the perception of the act *and* the interpretation of it' (IP 12). The other's behaviour, then, is experienced as meaningful and intentional only within a certain hermeneutic pre-understanding. So, in the case, for example, of a husband who begins to cry, one woman may interpret this as weakness, the other as sensitivity. In either instance, 'each will react to a greater or lesser extent according to a preconceived interpretive model' (IP 11).

Interpersonal experience is further complicated because, as an agent in the social world, my actions are ambivalent. In *Self and Others*,[1] Laing asks what definitively characterises an action directed towards the other. Is it the sincerity of my intention, or the intensity of their response?: 'In what sense do I do to the other what the other person says I am doing to him, if I do what I want, with other intentions, knowing, however, that the "effect" my action will have on him will be other than I intended, because *he* says so?' (SO 149). Does the husband who cries reveal his sensitivity, or does he betray his wife's need for masculine support? And, in so far as he correctly understands her interpretation, is he a man or a 'sissy'? In *Reason and Violence*, Laing's exegesis of Jean-Paul Sartre's *Critique of Dialectical Reason* (1960), this ambivalence is '*alteration*,'

---

1. *Self and Others* was issued in two editions, 1961 and 1969. The latter volume revises and expands the former. References in this chapter are to the first edition.

which 'occurs when my action passes from my-action-for-me to my-action-for-you' (RV 118). Though as physical processes, actions are quite determinate, as social realities they are inherently ambiguous. The primary reality of my action splits into two separate interpretations – my 'intentions' and the 'reaction' of the other. In the wrong environment, alteration is the means for what we now popularly call 'emotional blackmail:' children leave home despite their 'cruel abandonment' of a parent; wives 'selfishly' withhold care from their husband in order to work and educate themselves; the 'lover' who declares 'I can't live without you,' turns his partner into a potential murderer. Laing is wise to this dimension of 'alteration.' One of his exemplary little narratives in *Knots* runs

He feels she is blackmailing him
by making him feel guilty
because she is unhappy that he is unhappy (K 28)

As the power of emotional blackmail indicates, self-identity is inevitably affected by the alterity of my action; it is very naive, argues Laing, to assume that I am just who I take myself to be. In the jargon of *Interpersonal Perception*, this inescapable element of identity – 'how *I* think you see *me*' – is called 'meta-identity' (IP 5). Inevitably, there is no simple, given 'self-identity' which is not 'a synthesis of my looking at me with my view of the other's view of me' (IP 5). Another of Laing's 'knots' captures the way in which the other can 'inhabit' oneself:

Jack falls in love with Jill's image of Jack, taking it to be himself.
She must not die, because then he would lose himself. (K 31)

If, in thinking of myself, I inevitably interpret the behaviour of someone else, then I may, of course, deliberately act upon the other in order to induce a certain kind of recognition in his eyes. This is the domain of self-presentation so well analysed in the work of Erving Goffman. An alternative to acting upon the other, though, is of interest to Laing. One may engage in 'projection' – '*a class of actions whose primary object is not the other's experience of me, but my experience of the other*' (IP 15). Again, Laing reminds us, we are not in the realm of explanation, but of intentions and understanding: projection may be called a 'mental mechanism' but 'it is neither mental nor mechanical. It is an action whose intentional object is one's own experience of the other' (IP 15). If, for example, I want 'to be generous to someone who insists on seeing me as mean' then I may project upon them in order to 'render my meta-identity independent of the other' (IP 15). In *Self and Others*, Laing illustrates projection upon the other: 'A boy runs out of school; the mother opens her arms to hug him and he stands a little way off. The mother says, "Don't you love your mummy?" He says, "No." The mother says, "But mummy knows you do, darling," and gives him a big hug' (IP 147). As Laing points out, the mother simply abolishes the reality of the boy's experience of her in order to remove the disjunction between how the boy takes himself to be (not loving his mother), and how the mother takes him to be (loving his mother). Her ultimate aim, of course, is to control her meta-identity: the mother wishes to identify herself as loveable, and accordingly operates upon her experience of her son. This process may be more or less subtle: instead of being simply steamrollered (as in the above example), a spontaneous action may be treated as madness or badness, or wilfully misinterpreted (SO 151).

My experience of the other, upon which my self-identity depends, is therefore extremely complex. One of Laing's favourite sayings captures this complexity. In *Interpersonal Perception*, he remarks that 'the world of the adult, as of the child, is "*a unity of* the given and the constructed"' (IP 187). He clarifies this claim by a careful examination of my experience of the other, the source of my meta-identity: 'Peter's concrete experience of Paul is a unity of the given and the constructed: a synthesis of his own (Peter's) interpretations of his perceptions based on his expectations and his (Peter's) phantasy (projection), and of the distal stimulus that originates from "Paul"' (IP 19). Behind all these constructions, lurks the 'distal stimulus' of Paul himself, like a distant star emitting light.

Laing's complex account of interpersonal experience allows plenty of room for the various entanglements which might make sense of the schizoid position. In *Self and Others*, Laing describes a context in which alteration combines with projection in an unhealthy way. A patient lived with a paranoid mother who 'was always reading motives and intentions into actions that he originally felt did not have the ascribed motives and intentions' (SO 145). For example, 'if he cut his finger his mother would say that he had done so to upset her' (SO 145). After sustained immersion in this context, 'his "own" motives and intentions did get hopelessly entangled with those attributed to him' (SO 145). It is easy to extrapolate a schizoid response to this situation. How can this person be sure of what he is doing? Is he really in control of his actions? He assumes he is benevolent, but his malice is constantly revealed to him – some mysterious force seems to be working through him. If he is not to be this force, then he must withdraw from this interaction, and find a truer life elsewhere. If a physical removal is possible, then the only direction of escape is inward – by a contraction and narrowing of the self.

A succinct example of this withdrawal is also provided in Laing's autobiography, *Wisdom, Madness and Folly*. 'David' is a young man diagnosed as schizophrenic. His main personal relation is with his father, who bullies him, occasionally hits him, treats him like a housemaid, and otherwise regards David as if he were non-existent. David, though, is too ineloquent and too physically weak to stand up to his father; nor is he well enough to leave home and support himself. He must remain, despite himself, feminised, passive, and, all too often, depersonalised. How can he actualise himself in these circumstances in which he is imprisoned? David must respond somehow in order to 'live in this unliveable situation' (WMF 147). His solution is to change the self that he is. He constructs 'a completely imaginary world,' he 'withdraws from his body' – 'this place of rage, terror, desire and despair' – and no longer 'permeate[s] it with himself' (WMF 147). This process, of course, is not a 'mental mechanism.' As Laing makes clear, David's withdrawal from embodied existence is an intelligent and intelligible action: 'A condition and a process in which he originally felt himself to be the passive victim is *now* the outcome of his own action on his own experience' (WMF 148). By actively narrowing himself to an unembodied mental life, David has mastered his own situation, and maintained some kind of autonomy. Perhaps the only world he affects is one of ideas, but this at least is a kind of freedom.

The example of Julie in *The Divided Self* can also be clarified by Laing's later interpersonal analysis. Julie is a diagnosed schizophrenic who constantly repeats that she is a 'tolled bell' (or 'told belle'). She had been an extra-ordinarily passive child who would rarely express her own wishes, and who had, at times, to be given a list of instructions for her entire day. Julie's condition – 'ontological insecurity' in the terminology of *The*

Divided Self – may be translated into Laing's later interpersonal vocabulary. Laing records that 'Mrs X [Julie's mother] repeatedly emphasized
that Julie had never been a demanding baby. This did not mean that she
was not a generous person herself. In fact, she had "given her life" for
Julie, as she put it' (DS 184). If we apply Laing's later ideas to his earlier
work, then the interpersonal context becomes clearer. Mrs X conceives
of herself as generous, and this has a necessary impact on her relation to
her daughter. In order to experience her own 'generosity,' Mrs X
projects upon Julie a quite unjustified experience of complete satisfaction. Whatever Mrs X does is naturally and inevitably enough to satisfy
her daughter. Julie's extraordinary passivity is constructed as satiation:
'"She would never take too much cake. You just had to say, 'That's
enough, Julie,' and she wouldn't object"' (DS 187). What to Julie might
well have been stifling and repressing, is experienced by her mother as
the natural response to maternal generosity and self-sacrifice; on the
other hand, any autonomous demand from Julie would be reflected
back as malign ingratitude.

Laing's concern with these unliveable positions leads logically enough
to ways in which such situations may be concealed and mystified.
Directly articulated imperatives, Laing notes, are not the only means by
which the attitudes of others are expressed. In 'The Politics of the Family,' Laing outlines how, instead of asking or instructing someone to do
something, one may instead directly offer tokens of how that person is
experienced. So, for example, we find 'parents are themselves confused
by a child who does x, when they tell him to *do y*, and indicate he is x' –
an example of this might be the utterance, 'I'm always trying to get him
to make more friends, but he is so self-conscious. Isn't that right, dear?'
(PF 81). The instruction to make more friends is contradicted by the
identity which is indicated to the child. The child's consequent actions
undergo a double alteration: if he makes friends, he disappoints his
mother's expectation that he is shy; if he remains shy, he refuses the
explicit injunction to socialise more. In either case, he is a 'bad boy,' who
refuses to do his mother's bidding. As Laing notes, this is the classic
'double bind' described by Bateson and his colleagues (and taken up also
by David Cooper): the child may not even be able or allowed to make a
'metacommunicative' statement about the dual and irreconcilable alteration which his actions undergo.

R.D. Laing

Laing's discursive, polemical works in this period are accompanied by *Sanity, Madness and the Family*, a collection of case studies co-authored with Aaron Esterson. These studies of family situations flesh out Laing's argument that many so-called schizophrenic symptoms are intelligible responses to a particular social context. The case of 'Maya' is a good example. She is a twenty-eight year old woman who has spent many years as a hospitalised chronic schizophrenic. Amongst her symptoms are hallucinations, catatonia, depersonalisation, withdrawal, and loss of affect. The clinical interviews with Maya and her family, though, reveal a different story. She lives in a family where her own perceptions are constantly undermined. For example, even during interviews, her parents indulge in a constant series of non-verbal communications – the existence of which, however, they deny both to their interviewer and to their daughter. Maya is continually confronted with these communications, and with her parents' denials. Maya's parents also frequently deny her own self-interpretations. For example, when she began to have sexual thoughts about her parents, 'she tried to tell them about this, but they told her *she did not have any thoughts of that kind*' (SMF 26). This pattern of denial continued, 'She told them she masturbated *and they told her that she did not.* [...] *When she told her parents in the presence of the interviewer that she still masturbated, her parents simply told her that she did not.*' (SMF 26). This pattern of denial (and denial of denial) extends throughout 'Maya's memory, feelings, perceptions, motives, [and] intentions' (SMF 27).

Maya has to live with this peculiar world where fundamental truths are reflected back to her as illusions. Her response is to withdraw from herself. Since so much of her experience conflicts with her parents' denials, then she can find release by denying that her experience is anything to do with her: 'she herself disclaimed being the agent of her own thoughts, largely, it seems, to evade criticism and invalidation' (SMF 30). This repudiation was expressed in the classic schizophrenic 'symptom' of hearing 'voices:' these voices were her own thoughts, but they were ideas which she should not afford to have. Her withdrawal further extended from cognition into emotion and her own sense of embodiment – so as well as auditory hallucinations, she had a loss of affect, and a tendency to catatonia. But, as Laing and Esterson point out, these '"signs" and "symptoms" that are almost universally regarded in the psychiatric world as "caused" by a disease' are, in truth, 'the outcome of her interexperience and interaction with her parents' (SMF 32).

One objection which has often been made to the studies in *Sanity, Madness, and the Family* is that Laing did not publish a comparative study on families without a 'schizophrenic' member. This, it is presumed, would have enabled Laing to show whether disordered communication is a sufficient condition for 'schizophrenia.' Indeed, as Daniel Burston notes in *The Wing of Madness*, 'Laing and his colleagues came to the somewhat disappointing conclusion that the patterns of disordered communication they observed in the families of schizophrenics were often present in normal families as well' (WM 73). This might seem to sound the death knell for Laing's theory of the cause of 'schizophrenia.' However, we have to remember that Laing's intent is to *understand* 'schizophrenia,' not to *explain* it. That some individuals respond to their social context with 'schizophrenic' behaviour is, as Laing argues, intelligible. The simple fact, though, that some do not respond to similar contexts with 'schizophrenia' does not render the 'schizophrenic' response unintelligible. We return again to the fallacy of 'one-sided understanding' in which it is wrongly assumed that a meaningful relation is only real if it is universal. But this (as Jaspers pointed out) is patently false. If, for example, I am insulted to my face, I may respond with anger; another person might be indifferent; another might burst in tears. All these responses are equally meaningful. Similarly, one person might respond to a certain environment with a schizoid breakdown; another might escape, or fight back, or articulate the conflict. Laing needs merely to show that the 'schizophrenic' response is indeed, like the others, an intelligible reaction. In this aim, he is successful.

Normality and experience

Laing's interpretative analysis of personal relations shows how the self may withdraw from the body into a schizoid life. This happens, Laing argues, because of an inability to find satisfactory confirmation of one's actions and experience. One's potential is thwarted by the unsettling, disconfirming responses of others. Sometimes, as in the double bind, these stifling responses are inescapable – one can't even successfully conform, let alone rebel. An idea emerges in this analysis which becomes increasingly important in Laing's work: that of the construction of experience. The schizoid, as I have suggested above, is someone who constructs their experience in an unusual way: the 'I' is delimited and narrowed (by everyday standards) towards a domain of self-conscious and private mental representations.

Laing's work on the construction of experience derives some inspiration from his reading of the German philosopher, G.W. F. Hegel:

> The world, as Hegel puts it, is a 'unity of the given and the constructed.' It is difficult to determine what is 'given' and what are our 'constructions.' One way is to compare the ways people in different times and places, and even in the same time and place, experience the world. All of us have been, or will be, surprised, even incredulous, when we come across the data of anthropology for the first time, at how vast are the differences between ways of experiencing. (PF 82)

The distinction between the 'given' and the 'constructed' has frequently been of great concern to philosophers, even if only because discerning what is supposedly 'given' in human experience involves an enormous effort of theoretical construction. As Laing's anthropological reference indicates, however, the majority of his inspiration comes from empirical observation. In 'Politics of the Family,' for example, he elucidates further the boundaries of self. He foregrounds the distinction between 'inside' and 'outside' the (embodied) self by asking us to play a game with saliva. It is relatively easy to 'swallow the saliva in your mouth' or to 'take a glass of water,' then 'sip it and swallow it' (PF 92). But what, he asks, if one spits into the water and then swallows it, or spits out a sip of water and then drinks it again? Some people can do all these things readily, but many cannot. What operates is a culturally programmed distinction between inside and outside: 'there is a difference between saliva inside one's mouth, and that same saliva, one inch in space outside one's mouth' (PF 92). The distinction is more or less forceful according to material. For example, there is 'an even sharper differential in terms of faeces' (PF 92). The same might be said of vomit: what was, a few seconds ago, inside, is now revolting, though materially identical, because it is outside. A dog knows no better than to eat what it has regurgitated; most humans find this harder to do.

In fact, there is a whole range of experience and possibility that is delineated in an obstinate, yet contingent, way. The most obvious examples are the 'phonemes' – the minimal functional sound units – which we acquire as we learn a language. Consider the way, for example, in which the Japanese have difficulty distinguishing the 'r' and 'l' sounds of English speakers, or the way in which Scottish English speakers may find it difficult to discern the distinct vowels in the Standard English pronunciation of 'pull' and 'pool.' Even bodily movements are quite closely circumscribed: fold your arms, then unfold them, and then fold them the other way round. Many people cannot do this; others think they have done it, but have in fact merely folded their arms the same way as before.

What disturbs Laing in *The Politics of Experience* is the ease with which such constructions become inviolable and sacred; we naturalise what we are 'taught to experience, out of the whole range of possible experience' (PE 51). The problem is not so much that one is inducted into culturally contingent structures of experience; it is rather that the contingency of these structures is obscured, along with experiences which are anomalous to them. In order to psychoanalytically express this loss of potential, Laing creates a (potentially confusing) distinction between selfhood and ego. 'The ego is [...] an instrument of adaptation' – in Laing's view, what the ego adapts to is 'socialisation,' an attempt to make 'each new recruit to the human race [...] behave and experience in substantially the same way as those who have already got here' (PE 57). In this sense, says Laing, we have 'lost our *selves*' (PE 61). We no longer have selfhood because we have become alienated from our own shared constructions of the given: 'once certain fundamental structures of experience are shared, they come to be experienced as objective entities' (PE 65). If we adapt to them (as ego), it is because we have lost sight of our own role in creating these 'reified projections of our own freedom' (PE 65).

Laing borrows the term 'reification' from Marxist theory. There, this idea expresses the way in which economic 'forces' are (falsely) perceived as natural entities which exist independently of human institutions – as if stock-markets were storm clouds, and economics analogous to meteorology. In Laing's view, our everyday experience also reifies the constructions that we place upon reality. He argues forcefully that psychoanalytic defence mechanisms (such as denial – acting as if something never happened) are ways of eliminating anomalous experience, and then obscuring this activity of concealment. The ultimate aim is to expand the seeming 'given-ness' of experience until the constructions we place upon it can no longer be recognised as such. So, in repression, 'we forget something. And forget that we have forgotten it' (PF 98) (and so on, *ad infinitum*). Freud's talent, Laing implies, was in discovering the normalising operations in the construction of human sexuality: 'For instance, who ever heard of a good boy, and a normal man, *ever*, having wanted to suck his father's penis?' (PF 100).

For Laing, a dangerous aspect of normalisation surrounds the existence of groups. To a naive mind, the group is 'a new individual or organism or hyperorganism' (PE 76). Laing, however, is at pains to insist on a correct understanding of how groups exist (in other words, an 'ontology' of groups). A group, 'The We,' is 'a form of unification of a plurality composed by those who share the common experience of its ubiquitous invention among them' (PE 76). This sounds obscure, but can be easily clarified. For a group to exist, it is not enough that I merely conceive of its existence, with myself and some others as members. For a start, the others in the group must also conceive that it exists, and that they and I are members. Furthermore, they must communicate to me that they see themselves in this group, and that they see me as a part of the group too. I, for my part, must reciprocate, affirming my bond with them, and their bond with me. For every member of a group, 'I' experience 'you' experiencing 'me' experiencing 'you' and 'I' as a 'we.'

However, rather than decomposing the 'we' in this way, we may be caught up in what Laing calls a 'preontological phantasy' (PE 80) that takes the group as a real object for consciousness. In this case, 'the group becomes a machine – and it is forgotten that it is a man-made machine in which the machine is the very men who make it' (PE 81). This mystification, this phantasy, can develop so far that 'the relative permanence in space-time of patterns and patterns of patterns are what [we] must live and die for' (PE 81). Laing's analysis of groups inspires his discussion of international politics. Whether we are the West, the Soviets, or the Chinese, we phantasise that the inertia of groups is the stability of a real existent. This is particularly dangerous when this phantasy surrounds an alien group – 'the Other' (PE 78) – against which 'We' must unite. The 'Other' becomes the reason for our group's existence; it is a justification for the violence which we inflict on our deserters – if they are not for us, they are against us. Spell-bound by these fantasies, the group ethic 'one for all and all for one' is 'the ethic of the Gadarene swine [...] as we plunge in brotherhood to our destruction' (PE 79).

Laing's discussion of group cohesion and violence also expands into the sociological perspective pioneered by Scheff, Goffman and Szasz. Laing articulates the primary truth that psychiatric diagnosis is normative. The schizophrenic is regarded as a deviant, one of 'Them,' not 'Us.' As Laing later puts it in *The Voice of Experience*: 'any biological variations which may be found to correlate with experiential variations judged pathological will be regarded as pathological, because, and only because, those undesirable *experiences* were called pathological in the first place' (VE 43). Any reification of groups naturalises this normative judgement, and constructs an 'Other' – the 'mad' – against whom we must protect ourselves.

Furthermore, Laing notes, for some people labelled schizophrenic, the undesirability of their experience (to others, at least) consists in an 'immersion in inner space and time' which is 'regarded as anti-social withdrawal' (PE 103). In a different society, such unusual experience might not be regarded as deviant, and the attitude towards it could be more one of care and assistance. Laing's lengthy prose attempt to convey such experience, *The Bird of Paradise*, begins with a quote from the Apocryphal *Gospel of Thomas*, which emphasises the mystical loss of construction upon experience: 'When you make the two one, and when you make the inner as the outer and the outer as the inner and the above as the below [...] then you shall enter the Kingdom' (PE 140). Laing's interest in altered states of consciousness flows logically from his thesis on the construction of experience. As he points out in 'The Politics of the Family,' even the inside-outside distinction may collapse 'in ecstatic moments' such as 'making love, starvation, listening to music, high fever' (PF 92). This helps to explain why Laing should be so interested in LSD, meditation, and other forms of transcendental experience (including certain kinds of psychosis). As he remarks to Bob Mullan, 'was there a possibility if someone was stuck in a sort of a hell world

[…] that acid could release someone from being caught in this hell?'
(MTBN 226). *The Bird of Paradise* reflects a combination, therefore, of
drug induced as well as naturally created altered states:

There is one page in *The Bird of Paradise* that I don't think I could have written
without the experience of mescaline, which with some hesitation I put in and
incorporated […] in the text. But practically all of it was made out of my own
dreams and states of mind that I accessed between sleep and waking up from
sleep. Sort of altered states of consciousness, that with a bit of meditation you
get into. (MTBN 226)

These states of being free experience from static constructions, and
thereby reveal the human agency which creates them. Laing's way of
putting this is to say that in such experience, the 'centre of experience
moves from ego to Self' (PE 109) – in other words, from the adult state
of static constructions back to 'the normal range of imagination and
phantasy and reality that all children live in' (MTBN 226).

Laing has now come round full circle. As the foundation of 'egoic
experience,' and thus of adaptation to society, ontological security can
equally act as a mystifying veil which conceals our alienated human
creativity. Laing goes so far as to declare that everyday psychosis is 'a
grotesque travesty' (PE 119) of what madness could and should be. He
prescribes for us all a genuine madness which entails 'the dissolution of
the normal ego, that false self competently adjusted to our alienated
social reality' in order to achieve 'a rebirth, and the eventual re-
establishment of a new kind of ego-functioning' (PE 119). The false
self, implies Laing, can be dissolved by a loss of ontological security, and
replaced by a self that is conscious of its creative, structuring power.

In *The Facts of Life*, the idea of a rebirth becomes increasingly, and
implausibly literal. The psychotic journey, Laing speculates, may in fact
recall and overcome the vicissitudes of uterine experience. In the womb,
enquires Laing, 'What sort of reception awaits each new arrival
(zygote)?'; might not the experience of the fertilised egg 'reverberate
through all the generations of that first one of us all' (FL 31). If, as
seems likely, many children are unwanted, might this not explain why we
reproduce, as adult collections of cells, an unwelcoming environment?
Again, Laing analyses how one might withdraw from life. How does
there arise that 'heartless sentience' which is merely 'sensuality, the feel

of, without feeling *for*' (FL 33)? Might alienation of feeling result from an inhospitable intra-uterine environment which is recreated throughout life *after* birth? Could this explain why so few of us have a feeling *for* life? This train of thought leads Laing to one of his most unorthodox therapeutic practices – rebirthing. Laing was introduced to this, he relates in *The Facts of Life*, by Elizabeth Fehr, a psychotherapist who had been treating a psychotic, and had 'enacted with him his birth, playing the part of the midwife' (FL 68). Now, Laing tells us, this individual is 'working. Looks, moves, talks ordinarily' (FL 68).

The practice of rebirthing may well have therapeutic validity. After all, if a shamanistic rite-of-passage helps somebody who has been diagnosed as mentally ill, then it has succeeded (as a therapy, at least). Far more dubious is Laing's theorisation of rebirthing. He states, plausibly enough, that it is not '*a priori*, nonsense, or antecedently impossible, that prenatal patterns may be mapped onto natal and postnatal experience' (FL 57). It seems far from likely, though, that rebirthing actually operates upon expectations inherited from the zygote through generation after generation of cells. Laing provides little in the way of plausible argument: there is no striking empirical evidence for his thesis, other than testimony for which there may be a more convincing interpretation. Indeed, in *The Voice of Experience*, Laing retreats, perhaps not whole-heartedly, from his earlier argument that there is a direct mapping onto our adult experience from our pre-natal life. He claims merely to study the 'patterns which occur in embryology [...], in the human mind [...], and myth' (VE 109). We need not believe 'that a formal analogy itself betokens an actual real dynamic link between embryological reality and adult psychological reality;' the issue is more of 'variations of a theme' (VE 112). Nonetheless, Laing's career and reputation never really recovered from this excursion into what was 'pop-psychology.'

Conclusion

Laing's work does not offer a complete, coherent system of 'Laingian' therapy. A variety of different approaches are applied to a number of problems in living. However, there is a logic in the way his thoughts develop. The ontologically insecure individual has only a precarious sense of his or her own continued, individual, and autonomous existence. This fragility stems from a retraction of the self into the domain of the 'mental' or 'ideal,' a retreat in which the body may be left behind to negotiate with the shared, tangible world. This narrowing of the personality may be regarded not as some spontaneous 'insecurity,' but as an effort to deal with a social environment in which the self cannot fit. A schizoid life may, especially when it remains misunderstood and stigmatised, develop into a psychotic breakdown. Yet, even here, Laing sees some value. The psychotic constructs the world in deviant ways: he may, potentially, have insight into the constructive activity which takes place – un- or pre- consciously – throughout the everyday lives of the sane. If this is so, then the successful 'journey' through psychosis may provide a paradigm for therapy, rather than being merely a deviant experience which 'treatment' should aim to eliminate.

Later chapters will consider how Laing's ideas have been challenged, developed, or simply ignored. A question will now be posed which has remained largely unexamined by the wealth of literature on Laing. What relations and similarities are there between Laing's work and the philosophical and psychoanalytic thought of his home country?

Chapter Four

John Macmurray and the Divided Self

In Bob Mullan's collection of reminiscences, *R.D. Laing: Creative Destroyer* (1997), the physicist and writer Fritjof Capra recalls a conference address by Laing in which the latter criticises the scientific worldview. The problem, Laing states, begins with 'Galileo, who said that the scientific method was to study this world as if there were no consciousness and no living creatures in it' (CD 283); from this statement of method, Laing notes, there eventually proceeds an unwarranted presumption about reality: 'Galileo said: "Whatever cannot be measured and quantified is not scientific;" and in post-Galilean science this came to mean: "What cannot be quantified is not real"' (CD 283). And so, concludes Laing, 'Galileo's programme offers us a dead world: out go sight, sound, taste, touch, and smell, and along with them have gone aesthetic and ethical sensibility, values, quality, soul, consciousness, spirit' (CD 283).

Although Laing rarely acknowledges his local intellectual background, there are clear relations in his work to twentieth-century Scottish philosophy and its extensive criticism of the soulless world offered by science. This chapter will therefore be devoted to showing how Laing's ideas may be enriched by a virtual dialogue with the thought of the Scottish philosopher John Macmurray (and also with that of an earlier Scottish philosopher, J.B. Baillie). Macmurray was born in 1891, grew up in Aberdeen, and researched and taught in various institutions including the universities of Oxford, London and Edinburgh. By the time of his death in 1976, he had produced a wide body of work which argued for the importance to thought and experience of personal categories (as opposed to mechanical or organic concepts). His influence upon Laing has been noted by Macmurray's biographer, John Costello, who discusses Laing's membership of a discussion circle in Glasgow, the 'Abenheimer-Schorstein group' (named after two of its members, Karl Abenheimer and Joe Schorstein). According to Costello, 'Macmurray's works were read by the group because of his view of personal reality as constituted by relationships' (JM 352).

The reality of persons and of personal relationships is a constant, central theme in Macmurray's work. This chapter studies three stages in Macmurray's repersonalisation of experience. The first of these is the recovery of thought itself from objective scientific categories. Macmurray argues that scientific analysis cannot adequately describe thinking, and, since science is a species of thought, science cannot comprehend its own reality as a personal activity. Macmurray's next step is to repersonalise the self. For Macmurray, the influence of science upon philosophy has led to a depersonalisation of the self, in which only thinking remains as a personal reality, while action is relegated to an 'outer,' objectified self. Macmurray attacks the philosophical programme behind this self-division in order to re-integrate thought with action. The third stage is the repersonalisation of others: Macmurray argues that our primary kind of knowledge is acquired in a personal relationship of faith. These three steps in Macmurray's 'personalist' philosophy all provide fruitful analogies with Laing's ideas on both the objectifying tendencies of science and the formation of the divided self.

The boundaries of science

In *The Divided Self*, Laing refers to Macmurray as a thinker who criticises the depersonalising tendencies of the scientific, explanatory ambition 'to transmute persons into automata or animals:' 'it is difficult,' remarks Laing, 'to explain the persistence in all our thinking of elements of what Macmurray has called the "biological analogy"' (DS 23). The work by Macmurray to which Laing refers is *The Self as Agent*, the first volume of the former's Gifford Lectures; the lectures were published in book form in 1957, and were delivered a few years earlier in 1953. Since the interwar period, Macmurray had been advancing arguments against the increasing reach of scientific explanation. *The Boundaries of Science*, published in 1939 and based on Macmurray's Deems Lectures of 1936, provides his most detailed argument on the limits of scientific analysis. This volume is full of fascinating material (including a philosophical account of psychotherapy); the most relevant section for our present discussion, though, is Macmurray's account of scientific psychology, which he regards as proposing a 'theory such that if it is true, it cannot be true' (BS 130).

Macmurray points out that the search for scientific truth (of which psychology is a part) is a human activity with a certain purpose and meaning, and with certain conditions of validity. Yet these characteristics are precisely what a scientific analysis – like that offered by psychology – cannot capture:

> From the scientific point of view, all beliefs, including scientific beliefs, occur to people. The processes which cause them to occur are unintentional, and therefore, the beliefs are not the realization of a human intention to achieve knowledge. If the belief that all beliefs are brought about in this way is true, then, since it is a belief, it cannot be true. For to say that a belief is the product of the operation of objective forces which necessitate its occurrence under certain conditions, is clearly incompatible with holding that it is believed because it is true. (BS 129)

A clarification should here be offered on Macmurray's behalf; he is perhaps speaking loosely when he says that one cannot treat psychology as 'true.' Macmurray, in his Gifford Lectures, later offers a distinction between the 'truth' of a theory and its 'adequacy.' Psychology, in these terms, would not be untrue – good psychology is true psychology. However, psychology would lack adequacy to its object – the human personality – precisely because the activities of persons (including psychologists) cannot be properly appreciated psychologically.

This inadequacy is shown more precisely when Macmurray asks us to consider the hypothesis that belief is bound up with 'the activities of the endocrine glands' (BS 130). Though this hypothesis is, of course, outdated, the principle of Macmurray's discussion still obtains – one can, in effect, substitute any preferred biological mechanism. Macmurray asks,

> What is the psychologist who accepts [this hypothesis] to do? If he writes a book to prove it, he invites the retort that both his beliefs and the reasons he gives for them merely express the conditions of his own endocrine system, and that since mine works differently I cannot possibly be convinced, he will say. (BS 130)

Argument, notes Macmurray, has a powerful 'effect' upon our beliefs; but this 'effect' should not be understood as the product of scientific

causality. To psychologically understand argumentation (and by extension, other such human activities) is therefore to fall into absurdity.
Macmurray observes, for example, that, rather than arguing, a consistent
psychologist 'should rather be perfecting his techniques for modifying
the working of my physiological system in such a way that it would produce the same beliefs as his' (BS 130). To think psychologically about
reasoning is to reduce argument to a mere instrument, an epistemologi-
cal hammer, and a lightweight one at that, for, after all, there are more
effective instruments than words. This instrumental attitude would take
a consistent psychology beyond absurdity and towards an inhumanity
like that so brilliantly depicted by George Orwell in his dystopian novel
1984. When Winston Smith is tortured (or behaviourally conditioned, if
you prefer) by O'Brien, a member of the Thought Police, he finally
comes to 'agree' that 'freedom is slavery' and 'two and two make five.'

   The first step in Macmurray's repersonalisation of the world is
therefore to show the contradiction which arises if we assume that the
scientific, explanatory mode of knowledge is universally adequate.
Scientific activity, like other forms of thinking, can only be adequately
conceived of as a personal activity. Like Laing, Macmurray insists on a
clear distinction between understanding an argument or thought, and
subjecting it to the causal, explanatory analysis provided by psychology.

Repersonalising the person

Macmurray concludes that thought is a personal activity. Yet, because of
modern philosophical history, many other aspects of human being, he
notes, have been relegated to a non-personal domain. Because so many
philosophical doubts and conclusions seem unbelievable, there has
arisen a tradition of the division of the person. Our everyday practical
disbelief in philosophy is explained away by the influence of an
impersonal, alien, 'outer' shell which contaminates the purity of the reasonable conclusions reached by the 'mind.' In this way, large areas of
'embodied' personal life are, in fact, depersonalised by certain philosophers. This philosophical division of the self was noted also by Laing,
who saw it as a parallel to his own notion of the divided, schizoid self:

I developed an idea that I never fully developed in writing that, with the Descartian [i.e. Cartesian] split, the mainstream western thinking had developed a psychopathological streak. I thought that there was a curious parallel between the writings of psychopathology, which attributed a schizoid split between the self and the body or between the mind and matter, and the mainstream thinking about the subject. (MTBN 112)

To understand how this philosophical schizoid split develops, we need only briefly examine an argument from the work of René Descartes (1596–1650) and its logical extension in the later writings of the Scottish philosopher David Hume (1711–1776). In the Cartesian philosophy, the truth of our conclusions is assured by a particularly methodical kind of thinking. Descartes asserts that, in all the seemingly various modes of thought, we essentially follow a geometrical paradigm in which a set of implications are deduced from self-evident axioms:

Those long chains of reasoning [...] of which geometricians make use in order to arrive at the most difficult demonstrations, had caused me to imagine that [...], provided only that we abstain from receiving anything as true which is not so, and always retain the order which is necessary in order to deduce the one conclusion from the other, there can be nothing so remote that we cannot reach to it, nor so recondite that we cannot discover it. (DM 92)

Descartes' inspiration is mathematical and geometric proof – such as, for example, the conclusion from our knowledge of axioms concerning parallel lines, that the sum of the angles of a triangle, cannot, on pain of self-contradiction, be other than 180 degrees.

The insufficiency of this logical, deductive method even to scientific knowledge was later famously expounded by Hume. He recognises that to postulate the existence of a cause without its effect is not to violate deductive logic: one can conceive, for example, that heat freezes water, and though this is false, it is not nonsensical. Hume, though, rather than abandoning the Cartesian paradigm of axioms and logical deduction, argues that the apparent scientific knowledge of causality is in fact psychological, rather than strictly rational, certitude. He concludes that what is apparently knowledge of the world is no more than insistent opinion: 'Reason can never satisfy us that the existence of any one object does ever imply that of another; so that when we pass from the impression of one to the idea or belief of another, we are not determin'd by reason, but by custom or a principle of association' (THN 97). An expectation of a certain effect upon a cause is therefore merely an 'opinion' which 'may be most accurately defin'd, A LIVELY IDEA RELATED TO OR ASSOCIATED WITH A PRESENT IMPRESSION' (THN 96). Because of this disjunction between what is taken as rational belief in everyday existence, and what is rational belief when measured against the canon of Cartesian rationality, Hume implicitly divides the self. The essential realm of personality is a rational ego which believes only what is given by pure logic. The mind, however, is incessantly badgered by sensory thoughts. Some of these are merely muttered *sotto voce* – such as 'here is a unicorn', or 'carpets can fly'. Others, though, are bellowed at the mind: 'HERE IS MY ROOM!', 'FIRE HEATS WATER!'. The latter are the source of our pretensions to rational knowledge about the world. Belief in the reality of such substances as laws of 'cause' and 'effect' (and, indeed, other things and other people), is understood as a kind of endemic weakness of the will by which the person (implicitly equated with 'mind') succumbs to the impersonal forces of habitual opinion.

In the model of the self which emerges in the progression from Descartes to Hume, the real personality is a logically consistent ego which has lost hold of the reins which guide the body. The philosopher is therefore forced to limit his personal existence to a realm of thought. Only in this impoverished mode of being can he exist in rational autonomy. Macmurray, in his Gifford Lectures, provides an extensive critique of this divided self; and we may regard his arguments as a philosophical supplement to Laing's psychoanalytic account of the schizoid self. In the second volume of the Gifford Lectures, *Persons in Relation* (published in 1961, based on lectures from 1954), Macmurray notes the depersonalising split in the subject which is postulated in order to explain the gap between philosophical doubt (such as Hume's doubt about causality) and practical belief (such as our everyday trust in the regularity of nature): even though 'I refuse to act in conformity with my theory [...] and so provide evidence that I do not really believe it' (PR 130), I 'can always lay the blame upon the body and its practical demands' (PR 131). This get-out clause, argues Macmurray earlier, in *The Self as Agent*, is quite philosophically unacceptable. Such is our concentration on logical inference, that we also forget that 'belief – not theoretical assent – is a necessary element in knowledge. A logical system of true propositions does not of itself constitute a body of knowledge. To constitute knowledge it must also be believed by someone' (SA 78). In fact, concludes Macmurray, where belief is impossible, I cannot claim to have produced knowledge:

> Suppose that I am presented with a triumphant logical demonstration. I accept its premisses; I can find no flaw in the argument. The conclusion follows with logical necessity and is therefore logically certain. But at the same time I find the conclusion impossible to believe. What then? I can only reject it *in toto*, even if I can find no theoretical grounds for doing so. (SA 78)

This, for example, would be Macmurray's attitude to Hume's demonstration that scientific reasoning is not strictly 'logical.'

Macmurray's conclusion may seem shocking, even anti-rational. Does it not invite us to abandon rationality and to elevate dogma to universal truth? Certainly, Macmurray owes his readers a clearer account of the 'impossibility' of belief to which he refers. However, his conclusion simply articulates the attitude which lies behind philosophical debate. Philosophical problems, Macmurray implies, do not resemble problems in other disciplines. Take such classic philosophical conundrums as 'the problem of induction' or 'the problem of other minds.' It may seem that these are straightforward puzzles. How can we show that the future will resemble the past so that the laws of nature will remain constant even in experiences yet-to-come? How can we prove that there are other minds given that we have no direct acquaintance with another's experience? These problems might seem to resemble, for example, mathematical demonstrations. As we cannot deductively prove the validity of 'induction,' or the existence of 'other minds,' so, in mathematics, we cannot work out how to prove a particular hypothesis or theorem.

The resemblance, however, is superficial. In philosophical problems, we already have found the answer by a validated method. The *problem* is that we do not believe the answer that we find, no matter how logically inevitable it appears. Anyone who was happy to accept the philosophical 'answers' that we cannot know if the future will resemble the past, or that there are other persons, would not have a problem. That philosophical conclusions are experienced as problematic reflects their variance with our intuitive, already-given attitude to the world: reflection is confronted with stubborn intuition; the resulting 'stand-off' is a

philosophical problem. Philosophers, as is their wont, can forget that
this is the nature of a philosophical 'problem,' and so we have the situation to which Macmurray refers: 'Philosophers discuss with one another
how any of them can know that the others exist, and find no satisfactory
solution. We are so used to this that we no longer notice how comical it
is' (PR 21). Macmurray's observation on this lack of conviction – and
hence knowledge – applies, of course, to other philosophical problems:
the philosopher who addresses his colleagues on the 'problem of other
minds' will also draft an article on 'the problem of induction' using an
electronic computer.

The inauthenticity of philosophical doubt appears even more comic if
one brings in an appropriate comparison (inspired by Laing's
observations on the 'psychopathological streak' of 'mainstream western
thinking'). For example, the diagnosed 'paranoid schizophrenic' who
claims that other people are robots has merely arrived, intuitively, at a
conclusion toward which a philosopher must labour in a lengthy treatise.
Yet, what the madman lacks in logical articulation, he makes up for in
conviction. Philosophers save their sceptical conclusions for lectures
and books. A madman, however, will live his belief, experiencing in
every minute of his 'psychosis' the loneliness, fear, and contempt of one
who believes himself to be the only person alive in the universe, and
who perceives the inanimate human shells which emptily parade before
him. A madman is a philosopher who has the courage of his convictions
– this difference explains why the former is incarcerated, while the latter
is given a lectureship.

Conventionally this kind of absurd knowledge without belief would,
as Macmurray argues, be overlooked by a hypothetical division of the
self into active, theorising mind and passive body. Yet, argues
Macmurray, if we are not arrive at this ridiculous position, then we must
scrupulously investigate our premises. The problematic assumption, he
believes, is that philosophy should produce a theory by which to absolutely secure knowledge against error:

This, it may be said, is the point of view of philosophy – that nothing is known
until it has been transformed, by rational criticism, from a mere belief into a logical certainty. Knowledge, in this strict sense of the term, is the product of
thought and lies at the end of a process which begins in doubt. (SA 78)

Such is the attitude stated clearly by Descartes for example, when he laments his immersion in a body and society which have already provided him with an attitude to the world, a sprawling hodge-podge of assumptions and practices which have not yet been articulated and rationalised:

since we have all been children before men, and since it has for long fallen to us to be governed by our appetites and by our teachers (who often contradicted one another, and none of whom perhaps counselled us always for the best), it is almost impossible that our judgements should be so excellent or solid as they should have been had we had complete use of our reason since our birth, and had we been guided by its means alone. (DM 88)

Doubting everything that can be doubted, a kind of philosophical slum-clearance programme, is a habit of thought which originates in this assumption. The original aim was to leave some foundation stone that might reveal a necessary and sufficient criterion of knowledge.

Yet, notes Macmurray, if one abandons the search for such a foundation stone, then one is no longer enthralled to this peculiar philosophical compulsion to doubt (or claim to doubt) everything that conceivably can be doubted. Descartes sees the potential for doubt as a sign that a belief should be suspended pending theoretical revalidation: 'it was necessary for me to reject as absolutely false everything as to which I could imagine the least ground of doubt, in order to see if afterwards there remained anything in my belief that was entirely certain' (DM 101). Macmurray, however, in *Interpreting the Universe* (1933) argues that 'a rational belief is not a belief which is known to be certainly true. It is simply a conclusion which it is reasonable to believe' (IE 78); it is not 'the function of thought' to 'provide us with knowledge which is fixed, absolute and finally guaranteed' (IE 77). In Macmurray's words, 'if I find myself possessed of a certain belief, and know no reason for questioning it, I *cannot* doubt it; and if I could my doubt would be irrational' (SA 76). He concludes, as we have seen, that 'if I am asked to adopt the method of systematic doubt, I am invited, as a matter of principle, to pretend to doubt what in fact I believe' (SA 77).

Macmurray is not alone in criticising the Cartesian method. An earlier twentieth-century Scottish philosopher, J.B. Baillie, presents an equally forceful critique of both the divided, depersonalised self and the search for a foundational principle of knowledge.[1] In *Studies in Human Nature* (1921), Baillie insists, against the Cartesian position, that thought is not the essence of human being: 'Truth [...] is certainly not all that the mind in its varied life strives after; by itself truth does not fill the cup of life to the full. The mind feels and perceives, it acts and it adores; and for such activities, truth, in the sense just stated, is neither relevant nor satisfying' (SHN 226). Baillie therefore argues that thinking is pathological when detached from day-to-day life:

> while the procedure of thinking has its own peculiar laws and aims, as the laws of seeing are different from those of hearing, the function is fulfilled in connection with the whole scheme of the individual life, separation from which leads not to healthy development but towards disease and dissolution. (SHN 216)

The precise form of this 'disease' is the division of the self between a portion that lives in the here-and-now, and a remainder which infers unbelievable conclusions. Baillie is unlike most philosophers because he identifies the personality proper with the putatively 'non-cognitive' component. Nonetheless, the end-point is the same as that later described by Laing and Macmurray, and earlier suffered by Hume: 'the thinking agent is turned into a quasi-external spectator of his own processes, watching the revolutions of his intellect as it produces concept, hypothesis, and inference, and having neither the power nor the interest to participate in its operations' (SHN 215).

Baillie, in a throwaway remark, also neatly encapsulates another problematic dimension to the Cartesian project. He points out the insufficiency of a theoretical answer to the question 'what is truth?': 'the complete answer to the question,' he tells us, 'cannot be found by postulating a "criterion" of truth. A criterion of truth must itself be a true criterion, and we are thus at once in an indefinite regress in the search for such an instrument, or we already have it in our hands all the while' (SHN 14). What, of course, such absurdities indicate is the impossibility of the Cartesian attempt to methodically (re)generate an indubitable and higher standard of knowledge from the assumptions

---

1. Baillie was also an important translator of philosophical literature: it his 1910 translation of Hegel's *Die Phänomenologie des Geistes* (*The Phenomenology of Mind*) to which Laing, for example, refers in *The Divided Self.*

and opinions which we find ourselves amongst as we proceed in everyday life. If everything is in doubt until it has been (re)validated theoretically, then this applies all the more strongly to any principle by which we might attempt to validate this revalidation. It seems, then, we must be willing to accept what we already believe as knowledge, howsoever fallible it may yet prove to be.

This is certainly Macmurray's conclusion. Knowing, he argues, is a skill which we already possess before we attempt to theorise and articulate it: 'the distinction between "right" and "wrong," which is constitutive for action, is the primary standard of validity; while the distinction between "true" and "false" is secondary' (SA 89). To know is primarily to act rightly:

Knowingly to actualize one of a number of possibles, and in doing so to negate the others, is to characterize the act that is so performed as right and the others as wrong. Again, it is the doing of the action which so distinguishes between right and wrong, not a theoretical judgement which may or may not precede, accompany or follow the doing. (SA 140)

In fact, concludes Macmurray, 'that immediate knowledge of the world which is the effortless result of living in it and working with it and struggling against it has a much higher claim to be taken to be the type of human knowledge than anything that science either has or can make possible' (IE 16). This phenomenon of unthinking knowledge to which Macmurray refers is no more mysterious, one might say, than grappling with a Chinese metal puzzle. We may, if stumped, theorise by symbolising and analysing the puzzle geometrically. However, we can quite competently solve a Chinese puzzle 'with our hands;' in which case we act reasonably, though not theoretically. Our philosophical habit, though, is to treat unthinking actions as unknowing unless these actions are directed by theorisation. We are so accustomed to this that we may even tend to regard unthinking action as sustained by unconscious theorising: as if, in walking across a room, I was constantly, but subconsciously, inferring the continued existence and stability of the floor, the ongoing breathableness of the air around me, and so forth.

'Ontologically insecure person[s],' Laing writes, 'seem [...] to have come to experience themselves as primarily split into a mind and a body. Usually they feel most closely identified with the "mind"' (DS 65); one may therefore see the schizoid split as analogous to the philosophical division of the self into mind and body: 'the unembodied self [...] engages in nothing directly. Its functions come to be observation, control, and criticism *vis-a-vis* what the body is experiencing and doing, and those operations which are usually spoken of as purely "mental"' (DS 69). This is the philosophical and spiritual position attacked by Macmurray – a position in which mind and body are felt to be separate kind of existents, and in which my mind, my inner 'ego,' in some way communicates with my body, which is separate, distinct, and 'outer.' Macmurray's attack on Cartesian philosophy is therefore a way of re-uniting the self which methodical doubt has split asunder. If there is no conflict between philosophical knowledge and everyday, practical action, then there is no need to relegate the latter to an impersonal realm of 'bodily' existence. Not only, then, must thought be conceived of as a personal activity, but so too must the entire active, feeling (and thinking) human agent. This would be Macmurray's response to the potential philosophical argument that the 'schizoid' self is a philosophically logical, rather than a psychopathological, development.

Repersonalising others

To repersonalise our understanding of the self is one thing; it is another thing to restore personality to our understanding of what is outside of the self. After all, one might still attempt to know the world with only a depersonalising, objectifying attitude (like that criticised by Laing in the psychiatric propensity to explain, rather than understand, patients). Macmurray argues, though, that our immediate knowledge of the world is not primarily instrumental. Instead, the primary knowledge of a human being is interpersonal: 'the skills a child acquires, and the form in which he acquires them, fit him to take his place as a member of a personal community, and not to fend for himself in natural surroundings' (PR 58–59). The child's true environment is therefore the social world:

In the human infant – and this is the heart of the matter – the impulse to communication is his sole adaptation to the world into which he is born. Implicit and unconscious it may be, yet it is sufficient to constitute the mother-child relation as the basic form of human existence, as a personal mutuality, as a 'You and

I' with a common life. [...] Thus, human experience is, in principle, shared experience; human life, even in its most individual elements, is a common life; and human behaviour carries always, in its inherent structure, a reference to the personal Other. (PR 60–61)

To be knowledgeable is therefore fundamentally to have been socialised into the practices of a group:

the child's development has a continuous reference to the distinction between 'right' and 'wrong.' He learns to await the right time for the satisfaction of his desires; that some activities are permitted and others suppressed; that some things may be played with and others not. He learns, in general to submit his impulses to an order imposed by another will than his; and to subordinate his own desires to those of another person. He learns, in a word, to submit to reason. (PR 59)

Macmurray therefore finds a profound philosophical significance in the primary social relationship between child and carer: 'we may say that the first knowledge is the recognition of the Other as the person or agent in whom we live and move and have our being' (PR 77).

Philosophers, of course, frequently take theoretically validated explicit knowledge as the primary form. Macmurray argues that this dogma is so beguiling precisely because it proceeds from, and also further supports, an obliteration of communion with others. The primacy of the theoretical allows the philosopher to alienate himself from himself *and* from his existence as one person among many:

our fear of the Other generates the desire to escape from the demands of the Other upon us, by withdrawing from action into another life, the life of the mind, in which we can exist as thinkers, and realize our freedom in reflection. If this could be, then we should be pure minds, and spectators of a world of activity in which our actions would be determined for us by laws not of our making. In the realm of thought we should be free, but our bodily life would be determined by the laws of that world of necessity from which we have escaped. The world of action would become an *external* world, a world of phenomena; that is to say, a *show* – a dramatic spectacle which unrolls itself upon the stage for us to watch, to follow and to enjoy. (PR 130–31)

A philosopher of this kind consequently feels that she is answerable only for the thoughts of her logically rational ego, and not for the beliefs and practices of her putatively mechanical body: 'we have uncovered the motive of dualist thinking. It is the desire to know the truth without having to live by the truth. It is the secret wish to escape from moral commitment, from responsibility' (PR 131).

Macmurray regards this widespread attempt to evade one's original and primary social existence (which is later reflectively validated in a certain kind of philosophy) as essentially due to a crisis of faith which may occur during the development of a personal life. The divided self is, he argues, a consequence of the child's failure to trust his or her carer (designated by Macmurray as 'the mother'):

> If a child is to grow up, he must learn, stage by stage, to do for himself what has up to that time been done by the mother. But at all crucial points, at least, the decision rests with the mother, and therefore it must take the form of a deliberate refusal on her part to continue to show the child those expressions of her care for him that he expects. This refusal is, of course, itself an expression of the mother's care for him. But the child's stock of knowledge is too exiguous, the span of his anticipation too short, for him to understand this. (PR 88–89)

There is much – such as toilet training and times-tables – that a child must suffer in order to become an adult. Such things undoubtedly seem arduous at the time but, in retrospect, are recognised (by most of us) as a vital contribution to one's autonomy. A child has trust, or faith, precisely because, despite its inability to see the value of these formative experiences at the time, it nonetheless submits to them in order to maintain a relationship with a loved other. Macmurray's thesis is undeniably radical: he is, in effect, arguing against the whole Cartesian tradition, since he postulates that the primary kind of knowledge is fundamentally based upon a relationship of faith. Where this relation of faith fails, and becomes, at best, a prudent conformity, then, argues Macmurray, a partly depersonalised self will be created:

> He will become a 'good' boy, and by his 'goodness' he will create for himself a secret life of phantasy where his own wishes are granted. And this life of the imagination in an imaginary world will be for him his *real* life in the *real* world – the world of ideas. His life in the actual world will remain unreal – a necessity which he will make as habitual and automatic as possible. (PR 103)

Macmurray therefore aims to show how we can so easily overlook, for example, the absurdity of philosophical conclusions that are treated as knowledge but believed by nobody. Our propensity to treat some of our experience as alienated, as enmeshed in chains of natural causality, offers an explanation for the ease with which this style of thought has infected our culture.

However, Macmurray's ideas do diverge from those of Laing, despite their similar notions of a 'divided self' created by problems in personal relations. Macmurray, perhaps surprisingly, assents to a view of 'madness' as existing beyond the frontier of a personal relationship:

Let us suppose that a teacher of psychology is visited by a pupil who wishes to consult him about the progress of his work. [...] As [the interview] proceeds, however, it becomes evident that something is wrong with the pupil. He is in an abnormal state of mind, and the psychologist recognises clear symptoms of hysteria. At once the attitude of the teacher changes. He becomes a professional psychologist, observing and dealing with a classifiable case of mental disorder. From his side the relation has changed from a personal to an impersonal one; he adopts an *objective* attitude, and the pupil takes on the character of an object to be studied, with the purpose of determining the causation of his behaviour. (PR 29)

Whereas Laing would endeavour to hear the voice of a comprehensible intention, for Macmurray, the 'mentally ill' may only be explained in terms of psychological causality:

the objective attitude of the psychologist arises from, and is indeed made necessary by, the abnormal condition of the pupil. For the abnormality consists in his inability to enter into normal personal relations with others. This makes the personal attitude impossible in practice. More specifically, the abnormality consists in a loss of freedom – in a partial inability to act. The behaviour of the neurotic is compulsive. [...] The motives of his behaviour are no longer under intentional control, and function as 'causes' which determine his activity by themselves. This, at least, is the assumption underlying the change of attitude, the assumption that human behaviour is abnormal or irrational when it can only be understood as the effect of a cause, and not by reference to the intention of an agent. (PR 36)

This unwillingness to even try to recognise the intentional life of the mentally ill leads Macmurray into the same trap as many medical professionals. We might think, in this context, of the early psychologist or psychiatrist who essentially fails to recognise homosexuals as intentionally so, and who, instead, relegates their sexuality to a domain of psychological causality. There it may be treated by such means as hormonal supplements, the conditioning of reflexes, or by a complex replay of an early interpersonal relationship. Or, to take a more modern example, consider the family doctor who, unable to understand his patient, declares that her depression is not reactive (is not, in other words, a comprehensible form of sadness), and therefore prescribes the chemical intervention appropriate to an 'endogenous' depression. In both these cases, as in Macmurray's account, there is a depersonalisation of the 'patient' by an expert who is unable, or unwilling, to recognise the intentionality of the individual in question.

Laing is far from making such rash assumptions. He would regard as naive any attempt to objectify 'madness' into an effect of such causes as infantile trauma, conditioned reflexes, or chemical imbalances in the brain. Laing refuses to reduce the other to a baffling alien being who cannot be known or understood, but only explained in psychodynamic or neurological terms. The task is instead to acknowledge him or her in fullness and spontaneity. We might here recall Laing's famous objection in *The Divided Self* to the observations of a disturbed young man by the psychiatrist Kraepelin. Laing inquires, 'What about the boy's experience […]? He seems to be tormented and desperate. What is he "about" in speaking and acting this way? He is objecting to being measured and tested. He wants to be heard' (DS 31).

Why, though, with such a developed account of what is essentially a 'schizoid' condition, should Macmurray, as we have seen, treat the mentally ill as beyond the reach of understanding, and subject only to causal explanation? The answer perhaps lies in the essentially theological background to Macmurray's radical hypothesis on personal development. The parental carer is analogous to that all-loving God who, in his infinite wisdom, permits what to us seems to be suffering. Indeed, the torments inflicted lovingly on a child by her parents must seem as baffling to that child as God's command to Abraham that he offer his son Isaac as a sacrifice. This is why Macmurray asserts that 'the child can only be rescued from his despair by the grace of the mother; by a revelation of her continued love and care which convinces him that his fears are groundless' (PR 90). Those who, lacking a 'revelation' of the carer's 'continued love,' choose to remain divided selves are exiled from salvation; they are unable to recognise the gift of the other's grace; they lack suitable inspiration, and may only be compelled by earthly causality. For those of us who are not believers, and therefore perhaps more sceptical of the commandment to honour one's father and mother, Macmurray seems remarkably naive. That a child should have trust in adults is indeed vital; however, this trust is sometimes abused. The young are vulnerable precisely because they cannot easily distinguish between straightforward abuse and an experience which, although painful, is nonetheless a condition of growth and autonomy.

So, despite the similarities in their analysis of self-division, and, given Laing's acknowledgement of Macmurray, a likely relation of intellectual influence, these two thinkers diverge significantly. Laing seems more aware that self-division may be a meaningful way of coping with an upbringing where apparent suffering is not redeemed. This is why Laing cannot simply disapprove of the schizoid position. It may, like many so-called psychopathologies, be an adaptive response to a social environment which is far from loving. Consider again Laing's study in *Wisdom, Madness and Folly* of 'David,' a young man who has grown up in an abusive family, and who has developed into 'an ambulatory schizophrenic' (WMF 143):

In his teens he lives with his father. Father's girlfriend – physically naked – father and girlfriend make love with him around. Father sometimes loses his temper with him, hits him: he feels increasingly abject, cowardly, frightened. He decides to 'agree' with everything. He becomes compliant, dishonest, insincere, flatters, internally hates, externally fawns. (WMF 145)

David, who is being treated by his father as if were an unfeeling thing, can regain a sense of agency by cultivating his own Cartesian split:

His body: this place of rage, terror, desire and despair. This place of life, which is too harrowing and too fraught with too many conflicts and contradictions that entangle him, that he cannot resolve or transcend. What does he do? He withdraws from his body. He dissociates himself from it. He refuses to be it, live it, inhabit it, permeate it with himself. (WMF 147–48)

We might accept much of Macmurray's criticism of the philosophical tradition that legitimates the 'divided self.' Yet, as Laing seems to point out, there is a kind of rationality even in distrust: faith may indeed be necessary to human life, but (we might say on Laing's behalf) it should not be blind and unconditional.

Conclusion

Laing's thoughts on the depersonalised scientific worldview have rich parallels in the work of other twentieth-century Scottish theorists. By considering the work of Macmurray (and Baillie), we gain a sense of the fruitful dialogue between philosophy and psychiatry that undoubtedly helped Laing develop his ideas. He was not alone in criticising the objectifying tendencies of scientific explanation and the way in which they legitimate philosophically the divided self and depersonalised others. And, of course, a further point is emphasised: Laing did not spring fully fledged from an intellectual wasteland. He developed, rather, in a context of ideas that is today largely unknown. The shamefulness of this neglect of Scottish ideas becomes, as we shall see, all the more glaring, as we move on to consider the background of Scottish psychoanalytic thought. There, we shall find a psychoanalysis which insists – like Macmurray's philosophy – on the importance and reality of personal relationships.

Chapter Five

Scottish Psychoanalysis

It might be easy to assume that, before the appearance of R.D. Laing, psychoanalysts in Scotland made little contribution to the development of their discipline. However, this is a misconception. Scots have played a prominent role in the history of psychoanalytic psychiatry. John D. Sutherland (1905–1991), for example, was immensely significant in post-War British psychoanalysis. He was Medical Director of the renowned Tavistock Clinic in London from 1947–1968; he co-founded the Scottish Institute of Human Relations in 1970 (which today still trains psychoanalytic therapists in Glasgow and Edinburgh); and he edited and wrote for a variety of major psychoanalytic and psychiatric publications. Indeed, it was Sutherland who brought Laing to London, where the latter found a springboard to international recognition and fame (his eventual disdain for Sutherland notwithstanding).

This chapter focuses on two other Scottish psychotherapists – Ian Suttie and W.R.D. Fairbairn (the latter, in fact, was Sutherland's own analyst and psychoanalytic mentor) – who both made original, if nowadays somewhat neglected contributions to their field. In particular, I examine two theses which are evident in their work. The first is a rebuttal of the selfish and hedonistic aspects of the Freudian theory of value. The second thesis is still more radical: Suttie and Fairbairn find objections to the very notion of 'mental illness.' They argue (albeit more thoroughly in Suttie's case) that the distress treated by the psychiatrist should not be regarded as analogous to organic illness, nor thought of as a consequence of repressed instincts. They tend instead to understand the 'mentally ill' person as someone affected by difficulties in establishing social relationships, and who, because of these problems, may become yet further ostracised and marginalised within his or her society. In so doing, they anticipate Laing (and other anti-psychiatrists); they also, however, echo the earlier thought of the Scottish anthropologist William Robertson Smith.

The origin of love

Ian Suttie was born in 1889, and spent his formative years in Glasgow. From Glasgow University, he received both his Bachelor's degree in medicine and his MD. After a variety of posts in various mental health institutions in Scotland, Suttie took up in 1928 a clinical assistantship at the Tavistock Clinic in London. It is difficult to know to what extent Suttie's novel ideas may be attributed to his education in a Scottish context. As Dorothy Heard remarks in her introduction to the 1988 edition of Suttie's *The Origins of Love and Hate*, 'there are few clues that indicate how and from where Suttie derived his ideas' (IHP xx), and this is partly because

during [his wife, Jane Suttie's] lifetime there was no one in the family who had a specialist interest in psychoanalytic psychotherapy. This lack and her known desires, to live as far as possible unburdened by possessions and to 'die tidy,' may explain why no papers relating to any aspect of Ian's or her own work or life survive. (IHP xl)

However, despite these gaps in the evidence, Suttie's influence upon Scottish thought is clear. Macmurray in *Persons in Relation* explicitly refers, for example, to Suttie's argument against the assumption that the human infant is a mass of unsocialised impulses (PR 45).

The Origins of Love and Hate (1935), the only book which Suttie published before his premature death in the same year, might also, one imagines, have impressed Macmurray by providing something other than an empirical contribution to an established scientific paradigm. Suttie writes, 'The Freudians have all the advantage of a disciplined team working on the same hypotheses with definite conceptions and terminology. Against these advantages for interpretation and investigation, however, "team work" seems to hinder any critical philosophical investigation of basic assumptions' (OLH 5). Suttie therefore analyses the first principles of Freud's account of society:

The fundamental question we must ask ourselves is 'Is society a spontaneous expression of human nature, or an artifact of force?' Freud unhesitatingly and explicitly states that it is the latter. Society for him is maintained only by the dominance of the 'leader' over guilty and frightened 'followers,' just as social behaviour in the individual is (in his eyes) the outcome of repression by fear. We must of course remember the distinction between suppression by coercion, operating at conscious levels, and repression, which is entirely an unconscious process. In the process of socialization of the group however the two mechanisms operate 'in parallel' to produce somewhat the same result. (OLH 97)

Suttie is appalled by the extraordinary conceptual mess which Freud consequently creates in order to maintain the egoistic hypothesis (familiar from such early modern philosophers as Thomas Hobbes) that 'the goal of life is self-assertion and self-seeking, limited only by fear of unpleasant consequences or retaliation' (OLH 49). Freud's eventual account, to Suttie, is a tangle of 'supplementary theories and explanations which pile conjecture upon hypothesis' (OLH 33) through

such socializing forces as self-denying pacts, economic purpose, rational foresight, tenderness, remorse, sex desire, homo-sexuality, fear and authority, 'identification' and 'reversal of hostile feeling (envy)' – the last two themselves being hypothetical processes more difficult to understand than the phenomena they purport to explain. (OLH 115)

Suttie therefore argues that a new programme of research is required, and that it should proceed upon a reversal of Freudian theory. As part of this reversal, Suttie criticises the Freudian theory of the instincts. It seems more plausible to Suttie that instinctual gratification is not an end in itself; rather, whether in adult or infantile love, 'the emotions borrow, as it were, the *use* of organs [...] and turn them temporarily to purposes that are definitely social' (OLH 68). Thus, concludes, Suttie, 'it would be as absurd to regard the sex act as having a selfish "detensioning," evacuatory motive as to say that a woman desires maternity for the drainage of her mammary glands' (OLH 72n).

Such observations on the instincts profoundly challenge the Freudian account of emotions such as love. Freud starts from the premise that our primal, infantile aim is merely the pleasurable gratification which follows upon the relaxation of irritated tissues in organs such as the mouth, genitals, anus, and skin. His model of psychosexual development is a tale of how this initial narcissistic condition is lost. The mother, Freud tells us, conspires with her child's selfish gratification for a while, but eventually needs to get on with her own life. The father then enters the infantile consciousness as the agent who interferes with this state of

manifold erotic gratification. The child – or, at least, the boy-child –
overcomes his fearful jealousy of the father by identifying with him (this
is the famed 'Oedipal complex' and its resolution). In return for surren-
dering his autoerotic privileges, the boy will receive an adult sexual love
in which gratification is achieved through cooperation with another of
the 'opposite' sex. According to this theory, society's (necessary) repression of the sexual impulse leads, in the ideal case, to a useful perversion
in which sexuality is directed towards another person, and experienced
in an attenuated form as sentiment. In this standard psychoanalytic
model, feelings of love for another are therefore regarded as higher,
'sublimated' forms of sexual desire. Suttie only to an extent follows this
analysis. While he too accepts that Western culture (and some others)
repress sexuality, he does not believe that love is a consequence of
repressed sexuality. Instead, he argues, there is throughout Western culture a 'taboo on tenderness' in which expressions of non-sexual love for
its own sake are proscribed. Indeed, to Suttie, Freudian theory is indica-
tive of this taboo, for it treats such behaviour as touching, handholding,
and kissing as higher substitutes for repressed sexual desire.

Suttie clearly recognises that his argument is contrary to our cultural
prejudices: 'The idea that tenderness is a primal independent reality and
that it undergoes repression will seem untrue and even absurd unless
supported by much evidence' (OLH 80–81). To support his case, Suttie
points out the extent to which tenderness is, like sexuality, subject to
repression – and, in fact, may even be more thoroughly repressed than
the latter. Note, Suttie instructs us, how men may be perceived as
unmanly if they enjoy caring for babies. Such behaviour is instead
validated in substitutes such as care for pet animals; just as repressed
sexuality finds substitute outlets, so too does repressed tenderness.
(Though, as Suttie notes, working animals such as dogs are considered
more appropriate for men – the practical elements allow tenderness to
be hidden under the utilitarian pretence of a 'colleagueship of practical
interests' (OLH 84)). A further cover for tenderness, Suttie points out, is
provided by sexuality: sexualised love allows an acceptable, if narrowed
outlet for impulses of sentimentality – as if the hedonism involved is
accepted as fair exchange for the degrading display of emotion. As
Suttie puts it, 'we excuse tenderness or sentimentality in this case *on the
grounds of its sexual intention and tendencies*' (OLH 84). A further, cross-

cultural example, supports Suttie's thesis that tenderness may be subject to an independent taboo. He cites the anthropologist Bronislaw Malinowski's studies of the Trobriand Islanders. In their culture, Malinowski attests, it is more socially acceptable for an unmarried couple to have sexual relations than it is for them to exhibit tenderness through, for example, sharing a meal together. In such a case, the taboo on tenderness is explicitly stronger than the taboo on sexuality. As Suttie drily notes, 'if their civilization were like ours they would consider a res-taurant bill good grounds for divorce; the Sunday papers would print the menu and the Bishops would talk of the decay of morality' (OLH 92).

Suttie's notion of the 'taboo on tenderness' is a ground-breaking account of a widespread cultural prejudice against sentiment. Yet, is it really, as Suttie believes, an accurate observation on Freudian psychoanalysis as a discipline? Surely psychoanalysts, as dedicated observers of human experience, must appreciate that tenderness is an end in itself? Observers, however, often only 'see' what their premises allow – Suttie has pointed out the massive intellectual effort which Freud expended to explain away social phenomena. Indeed, so engrained were their habits of thought, psychoanalysts could be lead into outright absurdity rather than admit the independent existence of tenderness. A fine example of tabooed tenderness occurs, for example, in the work of the Vienna-educated psychoanalyst Wilhelm Reich (1897–1957). Reich is, it is fair to say, obsessed with the taboo on sexuality. In his study *The Function of the Orgasm* (1927; first English language edition, 1942) he asserts that 'people who are brought up with a negative attitude toward life and sex acquire a pleasure anxiety, which is physiologically anchored in chronic muscular spasms' (FO 7). Never one to avoid overstatement, Reich insists that 'psychic health depends upon orgastic potency, i.e., upon the degree to which one can surrender to and experience the climax of exci-tation in the natural sexual act' (FO 6).

Ironically, Reich's dependence upon a 'scientific' model based on the storage and release of energy ultimately leads to his notorious pseudo-discovery of the 'orgone' – a universal energy which supposedly permeates the material and organic worlds, and which is allegedly stored in the tense muscles of the sexually repressed. From 1936–1957, Reich conducted a correspondence with the radical, anti-authoritarian Scottish educationalist, A.S. Neill (1893–1973).[1] Reich's references to the orgone in these letters are quite delusional: knowledge of it allows him 'to determine the weather before any barometer in the world can do it,' and also provides 'the secret of cancer, rheumatism, tuberculosis, neurosis, psychosis and many other diseases' (RF 55, 2 April 1941). Yet, behind Reich's obsession with an all-pervasive sexual energy, there clearly lies a taboo on tenderness. The orgone is a way to square a mechanistic, selfish and hedonistic view of human life with the stubborn reality of loving human relations. For example, Reich notes in a further letter to Neill that

the contention of the psychoanalysts of the autistic character of the baby is an artefact. [...] The baby [...] if it does not find natural response to its outgoing feelings and emotions, in other words, if it is not understood emotionally in a simple manner and responded to, has to shut itself in. (RF 123, 6 August 1944)

The newborn, Reich observes, is not some infant solipsist interested in others solely as a means to its own hedonistic gratification. Rather, it is directly concerned to relate to fellow human beings – the gratification of its instincts by the carer is merely one amongst many markers of such a real personal contact.

Reich, however, would be unable to square this phenomenon with his basic energetic model; unless, that is, there were a special kind of energy which could provide a physical correlate to personal contact. This, of course, is exactly what orgone energy is supposed to be, as Reich admits when he discusses his relationship with his infant son:

It took me several weeks to learn to understand what the boy wanted when he cried. I did not apply any scientific knowledge – the more I did so, the less I succeeded. The only thing that worked was identifying myself with his expression and then I knew what he wanted. What psychoanalysis calls identification seems

---

1. Neill, who was born in Forfar and studied English Literature at Edinburgh University, developed a practice and theory of school education as the nurturing of 'self-regulating' students for whom learning was an autonomous activity, rather than a prudent response to a schoolmaster's punishments and rewards. His many books were widely translated, and his ideas were particularly influential in the USA, Germany, and Scandinavia.

to be rooted very deeply in what I might call the contact of the orgonotic system of a grown-up with that of the baby. (RF 123, 6 August 1944)

In a previous chapter, I discussed Laing's theory that psychotic beliefs may convey an existential truth that could not be communicated literally within a particular culture or context. 'Orgone energy' is exactly such a belief: to speak of interlinked orgone energy systems is really to speak of unselfconscious communion with another – an experience which, as Suttie (I believe rightly) notes, is banished from scientific and cultural visibility by a taboo on tenderness.

Although everyday Scottish culture is perhaps particularly keen on a 'hard-boiled' attitude which eschews sentiment, it is a credit to Scottish intellectual life that ideas of communion and tenderness did not have to appear in an encrypted form such as Reich's delusions. Suttie is not a one-off or a fluke: strikingly similar criticisms of Freudian theory are advanced by another contemporary, the psychoanalyst W.R.D. Fairbairn (who was also born in 1889, though he lived longer, dying in 1964). Fortunately for researchers, Fairbairn's life is much more fully documented; from it, we gain a sense of the philosophical influence upon his ideas. As David E. Scharff and Ellinor Birtles Fairbairn note in their introduction to Fairbairn's collected papers, 'before his medical studies, Fairbairn took his first university degree at Edinburgh University from 1911 to 1914 in what was formally called Mental Philosophy' (EI xiii). Scharff and Birtles Fairbairn regard this as an induction into an intellectual culture distinct from that of England:

The older Scottish universities were, for historical reasons, more closely connected with the development of continental European philosophy than with the intellectual ideas developed in England. Fairbairn was particularly influenced by Aristotelian psychology, which describes the social and political individual, and the tradition of Western thought derived from it, which emphasized the integrated maturity of men, for example in the philosophy of Hegel, which he studied at Edinburgh. (EI xiii)

It was in Edinburgh, for instance, that Fairbairn was exposed to the work of Pringle-Pattison: 'The metaphysical content of Fairbairn's first degree was strongly influenced by the interests of Professor Andrew (Seth) Pringle-Pattison (1850–1931) in the philosophies of Kant and

Hegel' (EI xiv). Indeed, even when Fairbairn taught psychology at Edinburgh, he was institutionally a philosopher:

After his medical qualification, Fairbairn taught in the Department of Mental Philosophy at Edinburgh University, where the syllabus covered the content of European thought from its origins in Greek civilization to the early twentieth century. [...] Since his psychology appointment was housed within the Department of Mental Philosophy, Fairbairn's duties included lecturing on the philosophical ideas of Leibnitz, Hobbes, Berkeley, James and Galton. (EI xiv)

As Judith Hughes notes in her book *Reshaping the Psycho-analytic Domain*, this philosophical bent – the questioning of first principles also apparent in Suttie – was not greatly appreciated by the English psychoanalytic establishment. Although Fairbairn was respected, his ideas were far from dominant:

To his London audience [...] Fairbairn's dissection of the formulations of those who he acknowledged as predecessors and his practice of proposing alternatives seemed to smack of hubris. That he was perceived in this light goes a long way to explain the cool reception his work, as well as his person, encountered. (RPD 17)

 Fairbairn particularly roused the ire of the psychoanalytic establishment by dismissing Freud's conception of the libido, that supposed fundamental sexual hedonism underlying all our diverse motivations. Like Suttie, Fairbairn believes that sensuous gratification is not an end in itself, but rather acts as a conduit for social relations. In his 1940 essay, 'Schizoid Factors in the Personality,' Fairbairn argues that the supposed Freudian stage of oral infantile sexuality is really the earliest form of communion between mother and child:

So far as the infant is concerned, the mouth is the chief organ of desire, the chief instrument of activity, the chief medium of satisfaction and frustration, the chief channel of love and hate, and, most important of all, the first means of intimate social contact. The first social relationship established by the individual is that between himself and his mother; and the focus of this relationship is the suckling situation, in which his mother's breast provides the focal point of his libidinal object, and his mouth the focal point of his own libidinal attitude. (SFP 10)

Fairbairn's vocabulary is perhaps unhelpful. The 'object' is not an inanimate thing; it is a person. His point, though, can be discerned through this professional jargon: the theory of 'object relations' offers a psychoanalysis based on personal relations. Conventional Freudian psychoanalysis is essentially mistaken, argues Fairbairn, in its understanding of the relationship between libido and its 'object.' The other person, or 'object,' is not a means to libidinal satisfaction; rather, the libido is a means by which to establish a relationship with the object. This point is taken up again in 'A Revised Psychopathology of the Psychoses and Neuroses' (1941):

> The conception of fundamental erotogenic zones constitutes an unsatisfactory basis for any theory of libidinal development because it is based upon a failure to recognize that the function of libidinal pleasure is essentially to provide a sign-post to the object. According to the conception of erotogenic zones the object is regarded as a sign-post to libidinal pleasure; and the cart is thus placed before the horse. (RP 33)

In Fairbairn's mature theory, developed in the 1940s, 'mental illness' is a result not, as Freud would have said, of the necessary repression of instincts, but of the extensive repression of 'bad' objects. When the infant finds its parents frustrating, it splits off the bad aspects of these objects, and preserves them in a repressed fantasy world, while, in the real world, the parents continue as idealised 'good' objects. What is unconscious to the infant, and later the mature adult, is the extent to which these imaginary bad others lurk 'inside,' draining energy from potentially fulfilling social relationships in the real world, and distorting both the individual's view of himself and his experience of others. The more pronounced this repressed realm of interpersonal fantasy, the more divided, the more 'schizoid' is the individual.

Fairbairn (again, like Suttie) is quite conscious that this revolutionary psychoanalytic account of 'mental illness' proceeds from a philosophical critique of the premises found in Freudian psychoanalysis. In the paper 'A Critical Evaluation of Certain Basic Psychoanalytical Conceptions' (1956) – later republished as 'Reevaluating Some Basic Concepts' – Fairbairn's philosophical vocabulary and indebtedness are perfectly clear:

Psychological hedonism for long appeared to the writer to provide an unsatisfactory basis for psychoanalytical theory because it relegates object-relationships
to a secondary place. Indeed, it involves the implicit assumption that man is not
by nature a social animal [...] as Aristotle described him in *Politics* [...], and that,
accordingly, social behaviour is an acquired characteristic. (BC 131–32)

Fairbairn's work, like Suttie's, is therefore also a political philosophy
directed against the assumptions of Freudian theory. With a theory of
sexual repression and the formation of a 'superego' (or conscience) by
the Oedipal complex, it seemed to Freud possible to explain how morality could be anchored in an essentially selfish personality. Yet, as
Fairbairn and Suttie note, a greater consonance with empirical evidence,
and a corresponding economy of explanation, is provided by a psychological theory that does not regard altruistic behaviour as fundamentally
parasitic upon selfish desires.

Their challenge to a widespread cultural prejudice sets Suttie and
Fairbairn against one of the fundamental assumptions of our modern
worldview: that altruism is essentially a secondary phenomenon, an
extrinsic manifestation of an intrinsic selfishness. The egoistic view may
treat compassion, for example, as a kind of prudent calculation in which
I act to avoid the compulsive imaginative reproduction within myself of
the suffering of others. Such a model assumes that my concern for others is essentially a selfish phenomenon: I wish to improve their lives only
in order to remove from my own the woes and pains generated by my
'sympathy' for them. Note, of course, that the means by which I do this
are indifferent: I may give as charity in order to alleviate my personal
discomfort at television pictures of Third World famine (a pseudo-
altruism based on *quid pro quo*); but I may just as easily turn off the television (a retreat into 'hard-boiled' indifference).

The taboo on tenderness leaves a void in ethical theory which is filled
by a seemingly natural conception of community, morality, and love as
constructions arising from selfish exchanges – transactions in which my
concern for the other's welfare is never direct, but is only an interest in a
greater return on my own well-being. This habit of thought is matched
in its stubbornness by the absurdity of the rationalisations that maintain
it. I once heard, for example, an intelligent and educated individual
claim that parents care for their children only in the hope that, one day,
their children will care for them. This analysis, I noted, would

presumably explain the grief exhibited by parents if their child should die: their investment has failed, their stocks have collapsed – why didn't they choose bonds, or bricks and mortar, rather than flesh and blood? Such bizarre mental contortions result from an enormous effort to deny that we may love others unselfishly, with a genuine concern for their welfare. Other than certain psychoanalysts, perhaps only theologians have managed to preserve this latter intuition in such notions as God's Grace, sacrifice without return, and a communion meal which really is such a thing as a 'free lunch.' Yet, of course, these theological intuitions are, to many, conveyed only in a form that is outside of rational discourse (a form which renders them as seemingly absurd as, for example, the 'orgone').

Future researchers might well ask, then, if a theological bent in Scottish intellectual life has helped to protect the concepts of love and tenderness, preserving them from complete theoretical dissolution in the era of social-contract theory, capitalist economics and utilitarianism. Indeed, as I shall show, this hypothesis becomes yet more likely when further ideas from Suttie and Fairbairn are examined. Anticipating R.D. Laing and others, Suttie and Fairbairn begin to ask whether the notion of 'mental illness' is anything more than an unhelpful metaphor. Furthermore, amongst other elements of their analysis, they begin also to advance a sociological account in which the insane are those who, for various reasons, are cut off from communion with others.

The myth of mental illness

Suttie's argument in *The Origins of Love and Hate* provides more than a *reductio ad absurdum* of Freudian egoism. Proceeding from the idea that human life is primarily social, Suttie also argues a strong case for the metaphorical character of the term 'mental illness.' What happens, he wonders, to the symptoms of 'mental illness' when they are thought of as the meaningful expressions of a social animal? Suttie persuasively argues that the most important and primary symptoms of incipient 'mental illness' 'refer in some way or other to the patient's relationship to other people – his social environment' (OLH 180). Loss of interest in people and the world, despair, anger, regression: these and other symptoms, insists Suttie, *'mean nothing but a disturbed social rapport'* (OLH 180). From these primary social symptoms there may issue those others – such as hallucination and confusion – which have no social meaning in themselves. These latter markers of 'mental illness,' Suttie argues, appear when the initial peculiarity of the individual 'becomes so extreme that harmonious mental cooperation with other becomes impossible,' a condition which arises when the tension between society and individual *'exceeds either the tolerance of the community or the patient's power of endurance'* (OLH 182–83). Suttie here moves towards a combination of models to explain 'mental illness.' In the early stages of insanity, the eventual patient exhibits deviant behaviour explicable by the taboo on tenderness: 'psychopathy' is, says Suttie, 'an archaic and (in [an] adult environment) inept attempt to improve love relationships' (OLH 201). For those who are particularly affected by problems in living with others, the deviance of their social life is amplified by their increasing ostracism from their community until, at last, having been 'sent to Coventry' they are sent to the psychiatrist (or the madhouse).

Suttie states a consequence of his model with striking prescience. Because 'mental illness' is, he believes, a cumulative disorder in social existence, it is only figuratively an illness: 'we can,' concludes Suttie, 'speak of mental "diseases" only metaphorically, since their nature and causes have nothing in common with, for example, a bacterial infection of a bodily organ' (OLH 183) – the analogy between, say, depression and diphtheria is licensed merely by the suffering occasioned by both. Indeed, as Suttie points, out, only a historical accident has made 'mental illness' the province of medics. The medical profession (rather than say 'the educator or the priest' (OLH 183)) took over the care of individuals so afflicted mainly because biological disorders could also produce behaviours such as depression or delirium. Doctors were accustomed to dealing with similar kinds of signs and symptoms, and could at least attempt to expand their explanatory approach into all such psychological phenomena.

In many ways, then, Suttie's analysis shows remarkable foresight. In 1935, he reaches conclusions like those so famously elaborated by postwar critics of psychiatry such as Thomas Szasz. Of course, radical conclusions were by no means commonplace amongst psychoanalysts in Scotland. Even Fairbairn, whose thought resembles Suttie's in many ways, could indulge in some strikingly complacent and repressive 'analysis.' This is evident in, for example, Fairbairn's 'The War Neuroses – Their Nature and Significance' (1943), which includes an account of a sailor whose experiences during the Second World War precipitate a 'war neurosis.' The patient experiences 'an acute anxiety state accompanied by incapacitating phobic symptoms after an oil-tanker in which he was serving as a maritime gunner was sunk by aerial attack' (WN 258). The specific traumatic experience arose when the sailor 'found himself grasped and pulled down by a drowning Chinaman who was a member of the ship's crew. In a desperate effort of self-preservation he gave the Chinaman a blow on the head and saw him sink back into a watery grave' (WN 258). Fairbairn's analysis is of the kind that gives psychoanalytic psychiatry a bad name (and would later, as we have seen, be mocked by novelists such as Kurt Vonnegut and Joseph Heller): the gunner is not anxious and frightened because of the guilt he feels at having killed an innocent man; rather, 'this [...] situation [...] functioned as a traumatic experience because, as investigation revealed, it brought to focus in an act of "murder" an intense and long-standing hatred of his father, which in the past had been deeply repressed owing to the anxiety and guilt attendant upon it' (WN 258). Sceptics will more likely conclude that Fairbairn's therapy attempts to persuade the gunner that his guilt is *really* Oedipal in origin, and that it is merely activated by an experience which reverberates with this repressed emotion. Fairbairn's psychoanalysis here functions as a comforting myth which casts a perfectly 'healthy' moral revulsion as an unreasonable and infantile anxiety. It postulates another world of emotions – the inner world of the Oedipal complex – through which seemingly everyday guilt reveals itself as a shadow cast by the radiance of infantile passions. What, of course, is lost to Fairbairn is the horror of a wartime ethos in which coping blithely with the killing of an innocent is regarded as normal and desirable. (The fact that, of course, many could cope with such an experience in no way establishes whether Fairbairn's patient really deserves to be regarded as 'mentally ill;' one might equally question the 'mental health' of those who can kill professionally.)

However, it would be unfair to see this unfortunate analysis as representative of Fairbairn's work. Even in comments which, to us, seem quite illiberal, he is capable of striking critical insights: 'homosexuality,' he writes, 'must be regarded, not simply as a perverse expression of natural sexuality, but as the natural sexual expression of a personality which has become perverse in its essential structure' (SOf 291). Despite this seemingly psychoanalytic jargon, Fairbairn himself recognises that to attribute 'perversity' to such a personality can only be to make an ethical evaluation:

in recent times there has been a widespread movement among psychiatrists towards the point of view that perverse sexual tendencies are 'symptoms' in the same sense as those which characterize the psychoneuroses; but this is a point of view which I cannot see my way to share. It is a point of view which arises out of a general modern tendency to substitute purely scientific standards for the moral standards of the past. (SOf 290–91)

Homosexuals, for Fairbairn, are therefore not ill; to say otherwise is to ascribe poor health when one is really passing a moral or ethical judgement. The homosexual therefore cannot be cured of a psychopathology, not because he is 'incurable,' but precisely because he recognises *consciously* that he is at odds with the mores of his group:

he regards his perversion as a personal asset [...] and any distress which he may display, if he falls foul of the Law, consists rather in fear of the forfeiture of social and material advantages than in any genuine guilt or remorse [...]. Basically, he despises the standards of the community of which he falls foul, and resents the attitude adopted by this community towards him. (SOf 293)

Although Fairbairn seems in his discussion to disapprove of homosexuality, he is at least clear – unlike many earlier and later psychiatrists – that such behaviour, *if* thought of as deviant, should be regarded as deviant ethically and not medically.

Indeed, for Fairbairn, even 'mental illness' proper may at times be understood as a conflict between the individual's ethos and the norms of the group to which he or she belongs, rather than as a matter of infantile 'object relations.' For example, the soldier who is classified as mentally ill is essentially also somebody, like the homosexual, who is at odds with the mores of his group:

the psychoneurotic solder has resigned his membership of the Army as a social group; and fundamentally he refuses to lead a normal military life within that group, albeit he justifies this refusal by suffering distress in virtue of which he feels unfit to do so. In similar fashion the sexual pervert refuses to lead a normal sexual life within the community. (SOf 292)

The difference, though, between an unabashed homosexual and a 'psychoneurotic' soldier is that the latter cannot represent to himself his own sense of alienation from the surrounding group (or, if you prefer, his problematic adult 'object relations'):

although such soldiers were still theoretically members of the Army group, they had more or less completely dissociated themselves from it. They were unwilling soldiers; and deep down in their minds they had motives which rendered a psychoneurosis preferable to normal participation in the life of the Army group. (SOf 290)

Rather than risk directly the wrath of his community, the 'mentally ill' soldier, for Fairbairn, develops a symptom which satisfies a particular goal – namely, removal from army life – without explicitly communicating this desire as his own. (In this, presumably unwittingly, Fairbairn echoes some of Suttie's remarks on the purposiveness behind the seeming passivity of 'being mentally ill' – Suttie, for example, points out the attractions to the hysteric of being an invalid (OLH 188).)

It is pertinent to note how far removed this analysis is from Freudian notions of 'mental illness.' The patient, Fairbairn argues, is certainly 'dis-eased,' but he or she is not, as with biological illness, the passive victim of natural causality. Nor, indeed, is such a person in thrall to the vicissitudes of poorly repressed instinct, nor even haunted by the ghosts of 'bad objects.' Rather, the 'mental illness' is an expression, though disavowed, of the agency of an alienated individual. The attribution of 'mental illness' is therefore misleading because it obscures the patient's intentional involvement with his 'symptoms.' Indeed, the patient will be cured precisely when these 'symptoms' no longer appear as alien intrusions into his psyche (i.e. as 'mental illness'), but as misunderstood expressions of his own autonomy. This account explicitly inspires the early work of Thomas Szasz, who, in *The Myth of Mental Illness* (1962), refers to Fairbairn's ideas:

Fairbairn [...] has been one of the most successful exponents of a consistently psychological formulation of so-called psychiatric problems. Emphasizing that psychoanalysis deals, above all else, with observations of, and statements about, object relationships [...] he has reformulated much of psychoanalytic theory from the vantage point of this ego-psychological (and by implication, communicational) approach. In his paper, 'Observations on the Nature of Hysterical States' (1954), he wrote:

Hysterical conversion is, of course, a defensive technique – one designed to prevent the conscious emergence of emotional conflicts involving object-relationships. Its essential and distinctive feature *is the substitution of a bodily state for a personal problem*; and this substitution enables the personal problem as such to be ignored [...].

I am in agreement with this simple yet precise statement. According to this view, the distinctive phenomenal feature of hysteria is the substitution of a 'bodily state' (Fairbairn) for communications by means of ordinary language concerning personal problems. As a result of this transformation ('translation') both the content and the form of the discourse change. The content changes from personal problems to bodily problems, while the form changes from verbal (linguistic) language to bodily (gestural) language. (MMI 90–91)

The symptom, for Szasz, is merely a way of expressing – while disavowing – an unrecognised emotion: 'Translation from what could be, or had been, ordinary language into protolanguage [...] makes communication concerning a significant subject possible, while at the same time it helps the speaker disown the disturbing implications of his message' (MMI 123–24).

Fairbairn's idea can be found explicitly in Szasz's work on the right wing of 'anti-psychiatry' (though Szasz, of course, would refuse this particular classification). Fairbairn's later work also has parallels, though, in the more left-wing scepticism towards 'mental illness' developed by Laing. The similarities have been obscured because a great deal has been made of Laing's connection with European thinkers through his induction into the 'Abenheimer group.' Craig Beveridge and Ronald Turnbull in their study of Scottish ideas, *The Eclipse of Scottish Culture* (1989), emphasise this Continental influence:

in the 1950s Laing was a member of a Glasgow discussion group which had a marked existentialist and personalist orientation [...].

This informal circle was sometimes called the 'Abenheimer group,' also 'the Schorstein group,' after its two Jewish members who had emigrated to Glasgow – Karl Abenheimer and Joe Schorstein. (ESC 110)

Beveridge and Turnbull show how this group deepened Laing's interest in continental philosophy: 'Thinkers discussed included Kierkegaard, Heidegger, Jaspers, Buber, Bultmann, Tillich, Sartre, Unamuno. Laing was a participant before moving to London, and read to the group drafts of *The Divided Self*' (ESC 110).

The Abenheimer group, however, were just as much in dialogue with local thinkers. As John D. Sutherland notes in *Fairbairn's Journey into the Interior* (1989), Fairbairn himself was a very significant figure in Abenheimer's Glaswegian milieu:

By the early 1950s, Fairbairn began to enjoy a much more congenial academic and professional atmosphere in Scotland. In Edinburgh the Davidson Clinic under Dr Winifred Rushforth had brought together a number of Jungian analysts, and in its Glasgow centre there were, as mentioned earlier, a few analytical psychotherapists including K.M. Abenheimer and R.W. Pickford, who was a senior member of the staff in the Psychology Department of the University. W.M. Millar, who had had analysis with Fairbairn, had become Professor of Psychiatry in Aberdeen. He established a notably psychodynamic climate in his group, as did T.F. Rodger, who [had] become the first Professor of Psychiatry in Glasgow. (FJ 142)

It was Rodger who helped create the climate in which Laing could begin his humanistic study of schizophrenia:

Rodger soon recruited to his staff T. Freeman, who had completed his training as a psychoanalyst in London while he worked in the Tavistock Clinic. Freeman was an enthusiastic researcher in schizophrenia, and there was an active group of young psychiatrists who became involved in this field, one of whom was R.D. Laing. (FJ 142)

This professional context, in which Fairbairn was an important figure, would seem to be at least as influential upon Laing as any informal philosophical group centred around Abenheimer. The latter, a Jungian, was rather scathing of Fairbairn's work (see FJ 144–50) – yet, it is Fairbairn's work to which Laing's own ideas are closer. This is particularly apparent in one of Laing's accounts of the genesis and meaning of psychopathological symptoms. Like Fairbairn, he argues that the personal experience of the world may greatly differ from that which would be conventionally attributed. For example:

Jill's mother had a stroke in 1963. She recovered to live on, nursed by Jill, until she died two years later. Jill said her mother had died in 1963. She did not recognize her mother in the woman she nursed for two years. When her mother 'officially' died in 1965, she felt relief not grief.

Thus official dates of public events can be out of phase with the structure of experience. (PF 68)

When the subject dissents from conventional constructions, Laing notes that others may simply refuse to recognise his or her feelings: 'Call experiential structure A, and public event B' – 'to preserve convention, there is a general collusion to disavow A when A and B do not match. Anyone breaking this rule is liable to invalidation' (PF 68). Again, like Fairbairn, Laing argues that this leads the subject to transform his or her experience so that these unconventional feelings are excluded from awareness: 'If our wishes, feelings, desires, hopes, fears, perception, imagination, memory, dreams … do not correspond to the law, they are outlawed, and excommunicated. Outlawed and excommunicated, they do not cease to exist. But they do undergo secondary transformations' (PF 74). This process of excommunication, Laing argues, is effected by defence mechanisms: 'We could never succeed unless we were able to employ a further set of operations on our experience to some of which I have already alluded. Most of these are described in psychoanalysis as "defence mechanisms"' (PF 95). For Laing, unrecognised feelings may be quelled by defence mechanisms which expel such emotions from conscious access and, at the same time, transform them into psychopathological symptoms. This thesis therefore almost exactly parallels that which can be discerned *in nuce* in Fairbairn's work: the individual, rather than face excommunication from his group (be it the family, the army, or society in general), excommunicates from himself those attitudes which would be considered inappropriate.

Thus, in Laing's philosophy, other people are a route through which fuller consciousness may be regained. This possibility, for Laing, can be seen from those accidental occasions in which the 'mentally ill' meet amongst themselves as autonomous individuals:

> The New Year is the biggest celebration in Scotland. [...] In Gartnavel, in the so-called 'back wards,' I have seen catatonic patients who hardly make a move, or utter a word, or seem to notice or care about anyone or anything around them year in and year out, smile, laugh, shake hands, wish someone 'A Guid New Year' and even dance ... and then by the afternoon or evening or next morning revert to their listless apathy. The change, however fleeting, in some of the most chronically withdrawn, 'backward' patients is amazing. If any drug had this effect, for a few hours, even minutes, it would be world famous, and would deserve to be celebrated as much as the Scottish New Year. The intoxicant here however is not a drug, not even alcoholic spirits, but the celebration of a spirit of fellowship. (WMF 31–32)

The genuine therapist, Laing argues, is therefore merely an expert in such meetings. True therapy begins with the restoration of a relationship in which the community recognises the authentic being of the patient – only this can give him or her a motive to return to the everyday world:

> This rift or rent [across the sane-mad line] is healed through a relationship with anybody, but it has to be somebody. Any 'relationship' through which this factor heals is 'therapeutic,' whether it is what is called, professionally, a 'therapeutic relationship' or not. The loss of a sense of human solidarity and camaraderie and communion affects people in different ways. Some people never seem to miss it. Others can't get on without it. (WMF 32)

This social distinction between 'us' and 'them' is one familiar from a tradition of Scottish theology and anthropology which long predates Laing. For example, in *Lectures on the Religion of the Semites* (1894), the Victorian social anthropologist, William Robertson Smith (1846–1894), discusses the rituals which establish group life. Pre-eminent amongst these is the communion meal:

> Among the Arabs every stranger whom one meets in the desert is a natural enemy, and has no protection against violence except his own strong hand or the fear that his tribe will avenge him if his blood be spilt. But if I have eaten the smallest morsel of food with a man, I have nothing further to fear from him;

'there is salt between us,' and he is bound not only to do me no harm, but to help and defend me as if I were his brother. (LRS 269–70)

Those who are outside of such communion are aliens; they are subhuman; they are animals who resemble people. The psychiatric division between the sane and the mad, in its unthinking exclusion of intentionality from the disturbed, is a modern version of this archaic distinction.

Robertson Smith's analysis seems therefore to echo throughout psychoanalysis in twentieth-century Scotland, and in particular in the work of Laing, Fairbairn, and Suttie. The latter concludes, for example, that the psychoanalyst relieves suffering by inviting the patient to return to society as a whole person:

the role of psychotherapy appears to be the restoration of the patient to full membership of society, to a feeling-interest integration with other minds, a rapport in which the patient can express himself in the confidence of evoking agreeable response and in which he feels himself able to respond agreeably to the overtures of others. (OLH 213)

Suttie, Fairbairn, and Laing are therefore connected not only by a common educational context, but by a shared philosophical questioning of the discipline of psychoanalysis. Their conclusions, as I have noted, contradict Freud's essentially egoistic view of the relation between the individual and the family: in Freud's theory, the family unit (like society in general) has no inherent value for the individual; it acts, rather, to impose taboos against selfish gratification in order to plant the roots of socialisation. Madness, in this system, is the unavoidable by-product of this induction into group life, and it may be treated by specialists whose methods transcend culture and history. However, throughout the arguments advanced by Suttie, Fairbairn and Laing, group life is an inherent part of human existence, and instincts are merely amongst the means by which contact is made with others. When, because of various circumstances, this contact cannot be made, then there arises the phenomenon of so-called 'mental illness.'

Concluding reflections

In *The Process of Change* (1982), the psychiatrist Maxwell Jones (1907–1990) discusses his work during the 1960s at Dingleton Hospital in the Scottish Borders. Jones, whom we may add to the list of neglected Scottish intellectuals, made an enormous and largely successful effort to liberalise the running of this previously hierarchical institution (and in this he might be compared to A.S. Neill, who did something similar for schools). Jones's therapeutic community stressed two-way communication, consensus rather than top-down leadership, and giving patients opportunities to exercise responsible freedom. In the introduction to his account of Dingleton, Jones explicitly relates his interests and methods to his upbringing in Scotland. As a Scot, Jones is both conscious of his group identity *and* of the value of autonomy:

> Blessed with a gifted and liberal family and living in a country which for centuries had fought oppression from its much more powerful neighbour (England), independence and freedom had a high priority in my value system. A group identity, whether home, school or country, far transcended the more universal values of money, power and material success. (PC 1–2)

As well as this emphasis on kinship and freedom, Jones was also drawn to psychiatric medicine not as a scientist, but as a humanist who had 'read widely in "classical literature" with its preoccupation with understanding the nuances of character' (PC 2). What he experienced in his training, though, was the objectifying attitude of the medical profession: 'the professors were on the whole coldly impersonal, dialogue and human relations were largely absent, and learning as a social process was entirely absent' (PC 2).

Ian Suttie, W.R.D. Fairbairn, Maxwell Jones, R.D. Laing: each is possessed of what we might, following the cultural historian George Davie, refer to as a 'democratic intellect.' In *The Democratic Intellect* (1961), Davie develops a thesis on the characteristics of Scottish intellectual inquiry – peculiarities which, he believes, have been both eroded and ignored. He argues that the native Scottish intellectual tradition, which to Davie was gradually suppressed by direct rule from London, was one in which 'the national taste for philosophy' gave learning 'a characteristically humanistic flavour' (DI 13). Thus it was usual 'in Scotland, in teaching mathematics and science, language and literature, to give an unusually large amount of attention to the first principles and metaphysical ground of the disciplines' (DI 13). Craig Beveridge and Ronald Turnbull restate and develop Davie's argument in *The Eclipse of Scottish Culture*. They too see a process of colonisation whereby a characteristically English theory of education came gradually, throughout the nineteenth and twentieth centuries, to dominate Scottish institutions. They contend that, following a 'compromise which allowed vestiges of the traditional approach to survive,' 'the ideal of a broad and theoretical education [...] as the guiding principle of the university system was [...] laid to rest' (ESC 82–83). Beveridge and Turnbull are, of course, not entirely pessimistic about the fate of this philosophical education. They believe that 'the Scottish bent for argument about first principles' (ESC 80) was only partly replaced by the 'down-to-earth, empiricist intellectualism' (ESC 82) characteristic of English inquiry. Much of *The Eclipse of Scottish Culture* is therefore directed to showing that the light of Scottish intellect has not been extinguished, but merely obscured by an educational establishment that refuses to record, interpret, or celebrate the achievements of its own scholars.

The thesis of the 'democratic intellect' has certainly had its critics. To some, it seems to impose a kind of litmus test for Scottish intellectuals, demanding of them adherence to a supposedly self-contained and uniform tradition, and misrepresenting the actual course of the history of ideas both in Scotland and abroad. It would indeed be wrong to think of twentieth-century Scottish psychoanalysis in this way – as self-sufficient and isolated. Suttie, for example, certainly knew well the innovative work of the Hungarian psychoanalyst Sandor Ferenczi (1873–1933): the latter's *Further Contributions to the Theory and Technique of Psychoanalysis* was translated by Suttie's wife, Jane Isabel, in 1926. Furthermore, such international relations did not always directly involve psychoanalytic ideas. Winifred Rushforth (1885–1983), for example, founded Edinburgh's Davidson Clinic for family therapy in 1939: part of her interest in personal relations was formed in India, where she observed the importance of mother-child contact in combating infant mortality.

However, Davie's account, and its successors, is written, like any other history, as a response to the present – a present in which intellectual specialisation and English cultural dominance have led to the neglect of philosophically-minded Scottish thinkers. And, although Davie does not discuss Suttie and Fairbairn, they clearly belong within this group: they are experts who scrutinise the first principles of their discipline rather than merely contributing, uncritically, to an established paradigm. By virtue of their comparative isolation from English psychoanalytic centres, Suttie and Fairbairn were able to protect and cultivate their own distinctive programmes of research. Their ideas can fairly be called 'Scottish psychoanalysis,' then, because their national position allowed them a comparative freedom from the psychoanalytic paradigms which had taken root in England. Ironically, the undue neglect of their ideas was in part also a consequence of their national location. Scotland gave Suttie and Fairbairn the space to develop, but not the power to propagate their ideas into neighbouring regions (or to adequately preserve them within Scottish institutions).

There are also, of course, reasons for interest in Scottish psychoanalysis which are broader than the attempt to overcome Scotland's national amnesia. A historian of ideas expresses the interests of the present: in this particular volume, I also try to show why today's climate of naively specialised and biologically oriented psychiatry should be confronted with an intellectual history that contains figures such as Fairbairn, Suttie, and Laing. Writing such a history is at times rather like mapping out constellations in the night sky. The patterns we see in the stars do not express real groupings, just as parallel thinkers like Suttie and Fairbairn may have had no direct contact. And as the absolute magnitude (or brightness) of a star is different from its apparent magnitude (its brightness as it appears to us), so dullards may shine intensely to their contemporaries, while those who are today's luminaries perhaps were obscure in their own time. Yet, histories of ideas marshall resources for a response to the present. Like a constellation, a pattern in the history of ideas may also give a valid bearing – in this case, towards the future. That there is a need to recover the work of R.D. Laing and his forebears, I shall demonstrate in the following chapter, where I discuss the ongoing struggle of what may be termed 'critical psychiatry,' the intellectual successor to 'anti-psychiatry.'

Chapter Six

Critical Psychiatry

The term 'anti-psychiatrist' was problematic enough for those to whom it was applied. For a number of reasons, the term has further fallen out of favour. 'Anti-psychiatry' sounds as if it were a wholly oppositional movement, but its arguments can often flow from a critical relation to an existing psychiatric tradition. I have shown the continuity, for example, that runs from W.R.D. Fairbairn to Thomas Szasz. A second problem with the term 'anti-psychiatry' is that it may seem to imply an indifference to the welfare of the 'mentally ill' – as if to refuse to medicalise such people were also to refuse to care for them. Undoubtedly the biggest problem, however, with the term 'anti-psychiatry' is its association with some extreme doctrines. I have already mentioned David Cooper's peculiar views on sexuality, and I have also discussed Laing's dubious ideas on pre-natal experience. The latter's tendency to romanticise 'schizophrenia' also imperilled the credibility of the anti-psychiatric enterprise. In arguing that 'schizophrenia' was a desirable state of transcendence, or that it was a potential healing journey, Laing risked overlooking the misery and danger (mostly to the sufferer) of psychotic experience.

Nevertheless, many of the criticisms made by Laing, his contemporaries, and his predecessors, continue to be made today despite a continuing entrenchment in the psychiatric profession of a medical model of 'mental illness.' The term 'anti-psychiatry,' though, has gone; the movement has, wisely, been renamed 'critical psychiatry.' This new term escapes the negative connotations of the old, and stresses that one can criticise psychiatry while still caring for those who are in distress.

The need for critical psychiatry exists because mainstream psychiatry did not so much absorb and synthesise anti-psychiatric criticisms, as ignore and belittle them. Consequently, anti-psychiatry has been the least successful of the countercultural movements which arose in the 1960s. Despite the advances made by feminists, and by gay and 'black' activists, the efforts of antipsychiatrists were rather less successful.

There can be little doubt that psychiatric stigmatisation and prejudice is more socially acceptable than racial or sexual discrimination. Derogatory terms for deviant, 'mentally ill' behaviour can still be used even in polite, reputedly educated circles. No English teacher, for example, would ever dare to refer to Jim the 'black' slave in *Huckleberry Finn* as a 'nigger,' but the use of the word 'mad' to describe Hamlet might well be regarded as acceptable. Even the polite use of 'mentally ill' as a euphemism for 'crazy' behaviour offers little improvement, since it simply transforms the 'madman' into a 'mad mechanism.' There currently seems to be no term which is both respectful of 'mad' people, and which also grants them intentionality and agency (as the term 'gay' for example negotiates between the straightforward offensiveness of 'poof' or 'fag' and the clinical tone of 'homosexual'). This failure in vocabulary is symptomatic of the ongoing marginalisation of the 'mad.' They are still deprived of civil liberties and treated as unintelligible aliens by both society at large and by the medical profession that is supposed to care for them.

Against medicalisation

Despite the efforts of anti-psychiatry, the medical profession continued to automatically classify and treat certain kinds of deviant behaviour, thought, and feeling as 'mental illness.' In *Mad to Be Normal*, Laing discusses with his interviewer, Bob Mullan, the impact his work had on the medical attitude to 'insanity.' Laing, perhaps too pessimistically, contends

my work has not made the slightest difference [...] There was a BBC programme a few years ago on R.D. Laing. They interviewed a number of psychiatrists about me and some of them made it clear that the main value of my work was to wake up psychiatrists so as *to refute it*. [...] To that extent, by acting as a gadfly, I had done a service in leading them to do more research as to the biological causation of this sort of disorder. (MTBN 378)

Laing's response is unduly negative. In Italy, for example, large-scale reforms of 'mental health' care and legislation took place. Spearheading the changes was Franco Basaglia, who was familiar with the innovations and theories of Goffman, Jones, Laing, and other anti-psychiatrists (see RDL-PAP 81–86). However, such successes were the exception rather than the rule: the dominant institutional approach to mental illness, today, is medical and biological. Is this because the established psychiatric approach has endured and negated anti-psychiatric criticism (from Laing, amongst others)? Or was the conventional response more of a dogma without dialogue?

As an example of a serious medical attempt to reply to anti-psychiatric criticisms, one might consider *The Reality of Mental Illness* (1986) by Martin Roth and Jerome Kroll. As their antithetical allusion to Szasz's *The Myth of Mental Illness* suggests, Roth and Kroll aim to provide a compelling scientific demonstration that, as they put it, 'the central arguments of antipsychiatry are simplistic' (RMI 30). Prime amongst their arguments is the thesis that anti-psychiatrists are, philosophically speaking, 'mind-body dualists' – in other words, that they believe the universe 'contains' both matter and spirit as two distinct substances. In a lengthy chapter, Roth and Kroll survey the history of philosophy, and conclude that 'the attack on psychiatry rests on the assumption that the mind-body problem has been solved by dualism' (RMI 52). In other words, Roth and Kroll suppose that only by separating off a separate, mental realm of being (the mind) can one argue that mental illness is a myth: for only then can there be a separate mental substance which might be distinguished from malfunctioning organic processes. On the other hand, argue Roth and Kroll, if we are not dualists, then we must accept that seemingly 'mental' events can correlate with, or even be reducible to, various altered biological functions – and this constitutes real 'mental illness.'

Their argument rests on a parody of anti-psychiatric arguments. I doubt whether any anti-psychiatrist has ever been so naive as to argue that the substance to which psychiatrists attach the predicate 'mental illness' is necessarily distinct, separate, and unrelated to bodily processes. The stronger argument, which Roth and Kroll fail to discuss, is that although various bodily 'abnormalities' may be found which correlate with 'mentally ill' behaviour, the premise that these functions are *malfunctions*, and hence *abnormal*, is a judgement which proceeds from cultural assumptions about what is normal and valid behaviour. Severe depression may perhaps be accompanied by lowered levels of the neurotransmitter serotonin, but that these levels are 'abnormally low' proceeds from the judgement that certain despairing moods are abnormal and should be corrected. One need not be a 'mind-body' dualist to ask whether this is a valid norm, whether an individual so afflicted behaves intelligibly (or may only be explained), or if it is right to compel someone to accept treatment for a condition they might not recognise as an illness.

Another, equally simplistic strand of Roth and Kroll's argument is to seek a scientific explanation for the norms which construct mental illness. Such an account would provide, they believe, a scientific way to demarcate mental health and illness (with, they confess, a vague boundary between two). As a preliminary to this effort, they contend that 'all societies throughout the ages have recognized the existence of insanity or mental illness among some of their members, and have distinguished these from conditions such as feeble-mindedness, criminality, and incongruent gender roles or sexual behaviour' (RMI 5). Now, in a simple factual sense, this is partly untrue: criminality, homosexuality, and cross-gendered behaviour have all been categorised as mental illness in the twentieth century. Even assume, though, that Roth and Kroll are correct, and that 'insanity' has always been distinctly recognised. They still fail to see that though such distinctions are perhaps universal, their content is quite variable (just as what is regarded as stupid, criminal, or sexually deviant varies from culture to culture). What today counts as anorexic, for example, might in the Middle Ages have qualified an individual for sainthood, and to the ancient Stoics, nothing was more laudable than an indifference to the body that would today be seen as 'schizoid.' Roth and Kroll believe, however, that one can extract a universal prototype for mental illness:

the indigenous descriptions of mental illness within very disparate cultures are extraordinarily similar and demonstrate the repetition of a few basic elements: incoherent speech, bizarre and idiosyncratic beliefs, purposeless or unpredictable or violent behaviour, and apparent absence of concern for one's own safety and comfort. (RMI 5)

Universally, we are told, there are people whose speech we don't understand, whose beliefs seem to make no sense, who don't apparently have motivations which allow us to predict their behaviour, and who act in a manner contrary to our notions of their well-being. Roth and Kroll, though, do not demonstrate that these people are all 'mad' in the same way. What is nonsense to one culture may make sense in another, or what is random and meaningless to one interlocutor may seem comprehensible to another. Roth and Kroll have shown little more than that there have always been people who are regarded as unintelligible; but that these people are necessarily incomprehensible is a quite unwarranted conclusion. What anti-psychiatrists have often tried to do is interpret and understand people who seem beyond 'sanity' – who seem, in Roth and Kroll's terminology, to suffer from a disease which creates a 'gross disturbance' in evolutionarily 'desirable' 'adaptive social behaviour' (RMI 71).

In their reliance on a universal 'sane-mad' distinction, Roth and Kroll also confuse the generality of a norm with its validity. To appreciate this mistake, transpose their error into the past. For example, in the eighteenth century, a democracy in which all adult women were enfranchised would have undoubtedly seemed an impossible condition to anyone who reasoned 'scientifically' from the available data: no society, past or present, occidental or oriental, allowed women to vote. Therefore, merely to parrot, in the twentieth century, the debatable belief that a sane-mad distinction has always existed is equally futile. Every society to which one may or may not 'adapt' has a future in which human understanding may render intelligible, perhaps justifiable, behaviour which in an earlier time seemed universally 'crazy.' This is true of all behaviour that is considered deviant in its own context: today's criminals, for example, may be 'resurrected' as wronged innocents in the future. Roth and Kroll want to 'futureproof' madness from such a possibility by presenting it as a timeless, biological deviance. Their response therefore merely repeats the mistakes originally exposed by anti-psychiatry – in particular, the error of 'reifying' deviance. In other words, Roth and Kroll treat a complex human activity as if it were part of a realm of changeless natural laws. They naively regard all identifications of madness as a normative superstructure built upon an underlying natural (perhaps evolutionary) process in human beings. Thus, as the laws of nature remain invariant, so too, claim Roth and Kroll, do the laws of mental illness: across all cultures, as through all 'human nature,' there is (supposedly) an underlying drive to identify and re-adapt those who are socially 'maladaptive.'

Roth and Kroll's work, flawed though it is, is at least detailed and sophisticated. However, *The Reality of Mental Illness* will probably never be read by the majority of practising psychiatrists. A more widely read (though implicit) response to anti-psychiatry is found in the introduction to the *Diagnostic Statistical Manual of Mental Disorders*, published by the American Psychiatric Association. Since 1952, DSM (as it is known) has provided a lengthy list of mental disorders with a set of signs and symptoms for each disorder, and a statement of how many and which of these criteria are sufficient for a diagnosis. Oddly enough for a catalogue of mental illness, the fourth edition ('DSM-IV') tends to assume that there is something wrong about saying that someone is mentally rather than physically ill. In the introduction to DSM-IV, readers are told (in a parallel to Roth and Kroll) that 'the term *mental disorder* unfortunately implies a distinction between "mental" disorders and "physical" disorders that is a reductionistic anachronism of mind/body dualism' (DSM xxi). The introduction goes on to say that whatever the pattern or syndrome that is conceived of as a disorder, it 'must not be merely an expectable and culturally sanctioned response to a particular event, for example, the death of a loved one. Whatever its original cause, it must currently be considered a manifestation of a behavioral, psychological, or biological dysfunction in the individual' (DSM xxi–xxii); so, DSM concludes, 'neither deviant behavior (e.g. political, religious, or sexual) nor conflicts that are primarily between the individual and society are mental disorders' (DSM xxi–xxii).

Though this definition tries to respond to anti-psychiatric criticisms, it does so by translating them into a pseudo-scientific language which robs them of their pertinence. Where critics of psychiatry would point out that human responses to a particular event reward a sensitive understanding that isn't one-sided, the DSM vocabulary speaks of expectable (i.e. predictable) responses which are culturally sanctioned. The model here is borrowed from the natural sciences. To take an example from Laing's writings: if grief follows upon loss, then this is because of a human predictability created by the 'forces' of socialisation. Where, however, there is grief with no loss, then we have an effect, a 'dysfunction' whose cause is internal to the individual (an 'endogenous' rather than a 'reactive' depression). Yet, as ever, the 'dysfunction' is normatively defined. No matter how much DSM-IV asserts that mental disorder is not deviance, the logic of its categories is all too clear. To DSM, anyone who deviates from conventional understandings of what they should be thinking, feeling, and doing, is suffering from an 'internal' disorder.

DSM and other classificatory schemes for mental illness arose after the heyday of anti-psychiatry. However, more recent critics of psychiatry have continued and elaborated the work of their predecessors. In *Schizophrenia: A Scientific Delusion?* (1990), Mary Boyle challenges the scientific validity of this paradigm psychiatric classification. Boyle notes, of course, the traditional antipsychiatric point that our interest in such disorders (should they exist) is normative: 'What psychiatrists and medical researchers [...] try to classify are putative patterns of unwanted physical and behavioural phenomena' (SSD 82). That such patterns should or should not be unwanted, by self or others, is an ethical question. Yet, there is another question which must be carefully investigated: how real are the patterns of behaviour supposedly classified by psychiatry? Boyle points out that, if there are indeed psychiatric syndromes worthy of investigation, then the criteria for these conditions must 'summarise a [statistically] meaningful cluster of phenomena, i.e. a cluster unlikely to have occurred by chance and therefore likely to signify other, as yet unknown, events' (SSD 11). For any investigation into causes to be properly founded, there must firstly be some *effect* consisting in a statistically significant pattern of co-occurrences. Boyle sceptically reviews a variety of psychiatric literature in order to argue that, in fact, there are no schizophrenic patterns such as those described by schemes – such as DSM – which postulate a statistically significant association of prolonged hallucination, delusion, and so forth, with a certain age of onset, and various other positive and negative criteria. As an example of her many counterarguments, consider Boyle's point that 'the psychiatric population, which comprises, after all, those who have been noticed and brought to psychiatric attention, will by definition contain more cases of co-occurrence than of single disturbing behaviours' (SSD 182). A pattern such as 'schizophrenia' is, to Boyle, a myth derived from an unrepresentative sample population – those who have more manageable experiences involving fewer 'symptoms' and 'signs' will tend to stay below the psychiatric 'radar.' Furthermore, once psychiatrists believe that such patterns exist, according to Boyle, they will tend to project them even onto patients who do not exhibit the full cluster of 'schizophrenia.'

A further criticism of the medical model so valorised by DSM and by Roth and Kroll is that it also almost inevitably leads to some form of treatment being applied, and such treatments are usually biologically founded. In *Toxic Psychiatry* (1991), Peter Breggin, another recent critic of medical psychiatry, points out the consequences of a thoroughgoing 'biopsychiatric' approach to mental illness. He notes ironically that biologically minded 'psychiatrists see their patients in what we used to think of as animal terms' (TP 160). The general consequence of such depersonalisation, argues Breggin, is the administration of drugs or treatments whose general harmfulness simulates a 'cure' of the psychiatric condition. He contends, for example, that antidepressants work not by correcting some putative chemical imbalance in the brain, but by having the same effect on 'mentally ill' individuals as on normal individuals, that of 'blunting the emotions and confusing the mind' (TP 211). Much the same, for Breggin, can be said about the prescription of Ritalin to 'hyperactive' children: 'Ritalin has the same effect on all individuals, regardless of their psychiatric diagnosis or behaviour,' namely 'sadness or depression, social withdrawal, flattened emotions, and loss of energy' – these side effects, believes Breggin, are the *primary "therapeutic effect"* (TP 378). Electro-convulsive therapy for depression, he argues, works in a similarly destructive way 'by causing an organic brain syndrome, with memory loss, confusion, and disorientation, and by producing lobotomy effects' (TP 245). As Breggin points out, electric shocks to the brain are only supposed to be therapeutic for depressives (and 'schizophrenics'):

if a woman received an accidental shock in her kitchen, perhaps from touching her forehead against a short-circuited refrigerator, and fell to the floor convulsing, she'd be rushed to the local ER and treated as an acute medical emergency. If she awoke the way a shock patient does – dazed, confused, disoriented, and suffering from a headache, stiff neck, and nausea – she'd be hospitalized for careful observation and probably put on anticonvulsants for months to prevent another convulsion. But on a psychiatric ward she'd be told she was doing fine and 'not to worry,' while the electrical closed-head injury was inflicted again and again. (TP 233)

At best, such 'treatments' can damp down the undesirable behaviour in question; there is, argues Breggin, no necessary insight into the aetiology or the meaning of what is 'treated.'

The biological fixation persists despite continuing experiments in non-medical care for those who might be regarded as 'mentally ill.' The most famous of these experiments with more hospitable places where people in psycho-spiritual crisis can work through their distress was Soteria House in California, which ran under the guidance of Loren Mosher from 1971–1983. Mosher offered a largely non-medical environment where non-professional staff supported diagnosed 'schizo-phrenics.' The results were impressive. Lucy Johnstone in the second edition of *Users and Abusers of Psychiatry* (2000) notes both the successes of the Soteria Project, and that 'subsequent projects run along similar lines produced equally impressive results; overall, about two-thirds of people newly diagnosed as "schizophrenic" recovered with little or no drug treatment within two to twelve weeks' (UAP 259). Mosher's project was not subsequently taken further in the US, largely, one assumes, because it was so at odds with the prevailing medical model of 'mental illness.' There have, though, been a number of similar projects which aim to avoid placing 'schizophrenics' in the sick role and administering potent drugs to them.

However, in many ways, the psychiatric profession, which is limited largely to trained medical doctors, is besotted with the idea of 'mental illness.' Attempts to demedicalise the 'mentally ill' run counter to both the philosophical prejudices of biopsychiatry (that biological explana-tion is fundamental), and to the personal values of psychiatrists (that they are there to help the ill, and so cannot stand by and do nothing for the spiritually 'sick'). These medical values are inevitably transmitted to professions surrounding psychiatry such as general practice, nursing, and social work. As an example of medicalisation in action, consider Gwen Howe's *Working with Schizophrenia: A Needs Based Approach* (1995). Howe, a retired social worker, is all for the 'mentally ill' helping them-selves – so long as they have *first gained insight into their illness'* (WS 180) after a process of diagnosis, treatment and recovery (or management). Those 'sufferers' who deny that they have a mental illness are, to Howe, as bad as those professionals who indulge in mere 'academic debate' (WS 173) about the reality of schizophrenia or who present a non-biological 'aetiology.' In the latter group, of course, resides R.D. Laing, of whom Howe is predictably critical. As a sign of Laing's conceptual confusion, Howe picks up a quote from an interview in which he confesses 'I don't think I could pass an exam question on what is R.D. Laing's theory. I was looked to as one who had the answers but I never had them' (WS 1). Howe misses the point: the more Laing theorises, or offers the answers, the less he can allow the mentally ill to speak for themselves, and the less chance he has to *understand* their experience. The possibility of understanding psychotic experience, though, is something that never occurs to Howe. Behind her medical model, lies the assumption that biological explanation is fundamental. In *The Reality of Schizophrenia* (1991), she asserts: 'Perhaps the profound resistance to [the notion of] a serious mental illness such as schizophrenia is that such denial is the final bastion in defence of the spiritual part of ourselves being something other than a product of our genes and the intricate working of our brain cells' (RS 96). Even in a strict explanatory view, of course, there are more causal factors than genes and brain cells. Howe's point, though, is simply to assert the primacy of causal explanation; and so she provides a vague philosophy to suit this explanatory prejudice: 'the mind is inseparable from the brain, and surely the most wondrous and perplexing part of a sophisticated machine' (RS 96). The complex argument about the difference between explanation and understanding, and how meaning and validity escape analysis in terms of causal 'laws' remains unexamined.

Howe's easy philosophical assumptions lead her to be uncritically enthusiastic about the medical model of mental illness. So much so, in fact, that not only does she recommend effective diagnosis and treatment, but also, as with any other illness, *prevention*. And, because of the frequent early age of onset of 'schizophrenia,' this means vigilant observation of young people for the early signs of an eventual illness. Here is an example of the behaviour that Howe believes should be rigorously checked-out:

Mandy, who is sixteen, has been behaving strangely for a couple of months. She is clearly desperately unhappy, she is avoiding her peers, she is snarling at the whole family but refusing to leave the house, she declines to sit down to any meals and grabs enormous amounts of stodgy food from the fridge (and she's always been so sensible about diet and proud of her figure). (WS 41)

Howe argues that a doctor would act quickly if Mandy had possible symptoms of cancer, so why shouldn't schizophrenia be prevented in a similar way? Yet, a family who interpreted Mandy's behaviour as possible early 'schizophrenic' symptoms would be a very sinister group indeed. A range of understandings of this girl suggest themselves, none of which would have anything to do with neurological disorder. Perhaps she thinks her friends are idiots, her family fools, and is sick of being 'sensible' and looking nice. What indeed would a medical examination achieve at this point, except to drive a further wedge between her and her family? Howe, of course, regards it as another suspicious sign that Mandy 'becomes hysterical at the implication that she should see a doctor' (WS 42). Yet, even if the girl could be coaxed along to her GP, there is nothing to diagnose. The problem – apart from Mandy's lack of consent to examination – is that there is no reliable clinical test for 'schizophrenia' other than being 'schizophrenic.' One could perhaps medicate Mandy, and then her behaviour might change, but so would anybody's on powerful 'neuroleptic' drugs.

Howe's ringing declaration that we should deal with schizophrenia 'with DETERMINATION, DEDICATION, and a little MEDICATION' (WS 181) is therefore a handy reminder of professional complacency. Here we have the ideals of the medical and allied professions: that spiritual crisis should be met with firm resolve by specialised experts who can dispense the necessary chemical, physical, or surgical treatments; inconvenient, impractical, and pretentious criticisms of this approach are merely a distraction from the urgent need for prevention, diagnosis and treatment. Despite the work of both anti- and critical psychiatry, the medical scheme of things is very effectively entrenched in the psychiatric and 'caring' professions.

Extending recognition (i): libertarian responses

Yet, to the medical motto of 'determination, dedication, medication,' there has developed a critical response based around the notion of civil liberties, employing, we might say, the ethical motto of '*liberté, egalité*,

fraternité.' The libertarian strand of anti- and critical psychiatry opposes
to the medicalisation of spiritual deviance a robust defence of the rights
of the individual. This response is, to an extent, independent of
questions of intelligibility and aetiology. For example, even if we find
someone whose experiences are irrational and unintelligible, and these
experiences are clearly correlated with some biological variation, there
still remains the question as to whether this person should be able to
refuse treatment. Consider temporal lobe epilepsy, a neurological condition which can mimic symptoms of 'paranoid schizophrenia.' What if
the sufferer finds his altered experience – revelatory, hallucinatory,
heightened – to be valuable, rewarding, and meaningful? Similarly, what
if one day, a 'smoking gun' for schizophrenia is discovered – some
distinct organic condition which pertains to all schizophrenics, and only
to schizophrenics? Suppose then that a treatment is offered which
would alleviate all signs and symptoms of schizophrenia to the person
to whom it is offered. Would 'our' disapproval of the psychic effects of
the schizophrenic organic condition allow us to compel the person to be
treated? How far can a psychiatric diagnosis be allowed to render individuals legally incompetent? One continuing criticism of psychiatry is
directed at the power it has to restrict civil liberties (under the guise of
medical treatment) to those who are considered unable, like children, to
give informed consent. A Jehovah's Witness may refuse a blood
transfusion, but a 'madman' may be compelled or pressurised to
undergo treatment on the assumption that he could recognise its validity
were he to be cured. (Of course, even if this assumption is ethically
acceptable, the curative effects of psychiatric treatment are, as we have
seen, the subject of dispute.)

Lucy Johnstone provides an example of how medicine may impinge
upon the liberties of someone who is, as Thomas Scheff would put it,
'residually deviant.' She refers to a British television documentary which
records the fate of 'John Baptist,' 'a black man who believes that he was
born white, that he is descended from the royal family, and that his sister
has been cannibalised, but he is apparently coping perfectly well with his
life' (UAP 231). Baptist does not accept that he is mentally ill, nor does
he want to be medicated, but he is diagnosed as schizophrenic, and
threatened with commitment. He is eventually forcibly medicated until,
as Johnstone puts it, he is a 'silent, shambling wreck of his former self,

with a heart-breaking expression of sadness and hopelessness' (UAP 232). John Baptist's beliefs may have been very peculiar, but he was neither a threat to himself or others; yet, such is our society's continued war on error, he is coerced into a treatment that, to use Johnstone's words, can be regarded as 'a punishment for obstinately refusing to regulate his thoughts' (UAP 232).

But although 'schizophrenics' are still relatively powerless, there have been striking instances of demedicalisation. The gay rights movement provides probably the clearest example of a libertarian demolition of psychiatric diagnosis. In *Making us Crazy* (1997), a book-length critique of DSM, Herb Kutchins and Stuart Kirk demonstrate in one of their chapters the normative, political basis of the so-called mental illness 'homosexuality,' which existed as a category in DSM until the early 1970s. The pathologisation of homosexuality had led, note Kutchins and Kirk, to a variety of putatively therapeutic approaches: surgical intervention such as 'castration' and 'clitoridectomy,' chemical treatments such as 'sexual depressants' and 'hormone injection,' and psychotherapies such as 'psychoanalysis' and 'aversion therapy' (MC 59). Accompanying each method of 'treatment' (or 'punishment,' if you prefer), was some theory of the origin and meaning of homosexuality, be it biochemical, behaviourist, or psychodynamic.

What rendered these theories and pseudo-therapies irrelevant was not some striking discovery of the genuine 'causation' of homosexuality. Rather, note the authors of *Making us Crazy*, 'the Gordian knot' (MC 61) was cut by 'the Stonewall Riot in 1969, when police and gays battled for days in the streets of Greenwich Village' (MC 61). As part of their growing political movement, gays picketed and disrupted the annual conference of the American Psychiatric Association from 1970–1973. Indeed, in 1971 there appeared 'Dr Anonymous, a cloaked and hooded psychiatrist who declared that he was gay' and that he was a member of the 'Gay Psychiatric Association which met socially but secretly during the annual APA meetings' (MC 67). By 1973 homosexuality as a discrete category was dropped from DSM classification, and so did not appear in DSM-III in 1980. It did linger on though as Ego-Dystonic Homosexuality, i.e. being troubled about a homosexual orientation, until that too was dropped in DSM-IIIR, the revised third edition in 1987. Of course, there was never such a category as Ego-Dystonic Heterosexuality to cover individuals troubled by only lukewarm, superficial homosexuality, accompanied by an intense and unwelcome attraction to members of the opposite sex.

As the example of homosexuality reveals, the creation of mental illness in DSM is essentially a delineation of normality and deviance by a professional group. Kutchins and Kirk conclude: 'The dispute over the inclusion of homosexuality in DSM was not about research findings. It was a 20-year debate about beliefs and values' (MC 36). DSM is, in effect, a tyranny of the majority, channelled through their representatives, the esteemed members of the American Psychiatric Association:

The developers of DSM assume that if a group of psychiatrists agree on a list of atypical behaviors, the behaviors constitute a valid mental disorder. Using this approach, creating mental disorders can become a parlor game in which clusters of all kinds of behaviors (i.e. syndromes) can be added to the manual. (MC 252)

Kutchins and Kirk's contribution is 'Excessive Motorized Speed Disorder' (MC 252) for those who travel too fast in cars, boats, and motorcycles, and get into trouble or danger as a consequence. Two feminist critics of DSM, Paula Caplan and Magrit Eichler, have proposed the category 'Delusional Dominating Personality Disorder' (MC 167) to cover the harmful behaviour typical of powerful men in important organisations. (Criteria include, note Kutchins and Kirk, a 'tendency to use power, silence ... and avoidance ... in the face of interpersonal conflict' and 'a tendency to feel inordinately threatened by women who fail to disguise their intelligence' (MC 168).) Perhaps, even, one could create a 'Psychiatric Opposition Disorder' for those who irrationally oppose the scientific claims of psychiatry, challenge the reality of 'mental illnesses,' and question the efficacy and desirability of psychiatric treatments. Such provocations, which emphasise the contingency of norms of psychiatric diagnosis, are far from frivolous: they should be compared to genuine DSM categories such as 'Oppositional Defiant Disorder,' which essentially allows a medical diagnosis for troublesome young people who will not do what they are told and are a nuisance to others (see MC 257–260).

Another libertarian challenge to psychiatry is presented by Jeffrey Masson in *Against Therapy* (1989). Masson, in a series of detailed and convincing historical analyses, displays the insensitivity and hypocrisy of the psychiatric profession. In a novel twist, though, he exposes the oppressive potential even in psychoanalytic 'talking cures.' We learn, for example, how Freud trivialised the problems of young Dora, who was sent to him at the bidding of her father. She was caught as a pawn in a treacherous affair between her father and Frau K., a family friend whose husband had attempted, as a kind of *quid pro quo*, to seduce Dora when she was only fourteen years old. As Masson convincingly demonstrates, Freud cannot escape his prejudices. He concludes that Dora's revulsion and despair at this situation arise from her hysterical repression of the sexual excitement consequent upon Herr K.'s advances. Freud then tries to convince Dora that she should have acted on this putative unconscious attraction and married Herr K. (after a divorce, of course). Unsurprisingly, Dora terminates her analysis with Freud at this point. Freud, although perhaps disappointed, finds gratifying evidence for his own theories: Dora leaves because she has irrationally transferred onto Freud her dislike of Herr K. (see AT 84–114).

Freud's relationship with Dora, for Masson, exemplifies the failings of even the best-intended psychotherapy. The problem, as Masson sees it, is that any attempt to make someone 'better' requires a value-laden judgement by the therapist that their patient is, in fact, in a bad condition, and should be 'improved' by undergoing a therapeutic relationship. In such a relationship, Masson points out, 'no psychotherapist can avoid instilling or attempting to instil his or her values in patients' (AT 294). Indeed, even if the patient freely asks to be 'rectified,' the therapist still implicitly assents to and validates the patient's own self-estimation. The therapist therefore either takes liberty away from the patient, or conspires in the patient's own abdication of freedom. Masson regards this normative background to therapy as inherently sinister: 'Once we give *anybody* the right to decide who or what is normal and abnormal we have abdicated a fundamental intellectual responsibility to repudiate the very idea of making such distinctions' (AT 298).

Whereas a biologically oriented psychiatrist might miss the normative context of diagnosis, Masson is keenly aware of the value judgements involved, the fallibility of the expert, and the potential for abuse. Yet, of course, Masson has his own values – for he thinks it wrong to tell other people how they should feel about themselves. If, as Masson argues, the deviant individual should not be brought into line psychiatrically, then this too is a value-judgement. As Lucy Johnstone has noted (with reference to counselling) 'Western culture [...] inevitably incorporates values such as individual autonomy, responsibility, self-development and achievement which are not universally shared' (AT 254). Even to refrain from offering psychotherapy is therefore to decide, for someone else, what is right or wrong (and hence what is normal or abnormal) – the potential patient may not agree that he or she should be left alone. One could therefore equally argue that the demand for autonomy and self-creation is itself a value 'imposed' upon others, and that individualism is an institution from which some individuals may dissent. In truth, any attempt to help others (even by standing back so that they can help themselves) is inevitably laden with values. However, one can at least ask others whether they would prefer to be helped, or to be left alone: this though, requires a further assumption – that the person in question is capable of deciding his or her interests. Libertarian approaches, successful though they have been in cutting through the 'Gordian knot' of explanation, tend to be insufficient without some extra understanding of the so-called 'mentally ill.'

The continuing work of Thomas Szasz is a fine example of these limits. As Szasz's career has developed from the 1960s onward, he has made less and less reference to how one might understand the phenomena of 'mental illness.' Correspondingly, there is an increased emphasis on the freedom and responsibility which Szasz perceives in the thought, actions and feelings of the so-called 'insane.' With increasing frequency, Szasz's writings tip over into an almost inhuman libertarianism. For example, in *Insanity: The Idea and its Consequences* (1987), Szasz takes his insistence on the intentionality of the 'mentally ill' to its extreme:

When an Irish Republican Army prisoner in a British jail starves himself, no one claims that he suffers from *anorexia politica* and that his self-starvation is anything other than a personal choice; however, when a young woman in America starves herself, psychiatrists claim – and everyone concurs – that she suffers from *anorexia nervosa* and that her self-starvation is not a personal choice but the result of a serious mental illness. (I 201).

Of course, with this thought comes also the corollary that to force-feed, or otherwise attempt to eliminate anorexia without the sufferer's consent, is an infringement of the patient's civil liberties. Similar points can be made about 'schizophrenics' who intend to harm themselves or others, or depressives who are contemplating suicide.

Szasz is so keen to demedicalise 'mental illness' that, in so doing, he automatically restores full responsibility to affected individuals. However, there are other ways, one might say, of not being responsible for one's actions, other than being compelled by some kind of biological causality. After all, if I am constantly harangued by a terrifying voice which instructs me to poison other people's food, and I have had little or no experience of disobeying this voice, then I am under a kind of psychological duress. Similarly, if I believe falsely that I am overweight, and therefore starve myself, then my responsibility is also limited because I do not judge correctly the reality of my bodily condition. A similar point can be made about depressives who seem to find the world bleak and meaningless, and yet have no appreciable reason for so doing. Szasz does little to address these inner experiences of 'mental illness.' He generally forces all such phenomena into his role-playing, transactional paradigm, where illness or suffering is dissimulated in an act of instinctive cunning so that some benefit may accrue to the presumed sufferer. In other words, Szasz regards 'mental illness' as another side-effect of the Christian ethic of compassion criticised by Nietzsche – in a culture where compassion (rather than, say, freedom) is highly valued, power will accrue to those who are weak, ugly, disadvantaged, or sly enough to pretend to be so.

Yet, given the enormous disadvantages which surround those who are 'mentally ill,' one really has to wonder about this supposed forgery of signs and symptoms by the mentally ill. It seems far more likely that the 'mentally ill' lack self-understanding – something that even Szasz must suppose if their dissimulation is 'unconscious.' And, without self-understanding, it is hard to see how anyone can choose in their own interest. Someone who lacks self-understanding, though still capable of deciding and choosing, has limited responsibility precisely because they cannot properly represent to themselves their own motives and experiences, and indeed may even experience objective and interpersonal realities only in a form distorted by their own limited self-awareness. It is precisely because such people cannot understand themselves that they seem unintelligible to others; and it is precisely the psychiatrist's task, as Laing so often argued, to assist in their self-interpretation.

Extending recognition (ii): developing understanding

Although libertarian arguments against psychiatric diagnosis and treatment are powerful, they are strongest when they relate to questions of lifestyle or of emotion. One may well have a right to be gay, but what of human conditions in which reasonable thought itself seems to be impaired? A paradigm of such states (which might include anorexia and depression) is the clutch of behaviours denoted 'schizophrenia.' Here we seem to have a deviance not just of action and feeling, but of thought itself. Merely to assert a right to be 'schizophrenic' is therefore to leave open an alley of opposition. It could be responded that the 'schizophrenic's' unregulated thoughts mean that he or she is legally incompetent to exercise basic rights – just as a child is too cognitively immature to be given the right to decide everything for him- or herself.

Critical psychiatry must therefore respond to the further implication of the term 'mental illness' that the mind is disordered – that, in certain conditions, the sufferer possesses a broken mind which shows its malfunction in behaviour that is beyond the bounds of reason and understanding. If critical psychiatry can dispute this attribution, then it can begin to counteract the pathologisation of such behaviour. Of course, this opposition would also then assist a libertarian case: if my behaviour is intelligible, then my mind is perhaps sound enough for me to consider my own interests and to decide things for myself. Laing made one of the major steps along this road in *The Divided Self,* where he showed how psychotic experience could be understood as 'ontological insecurity' – a condition where one's existence as an embodied, distinct, and enduring person seems continually under threat. A similar ambition also underlay the studies in *Sanity, Madness and the Family,* where seemingly schizophrenic behaviour was, once put in its familial context, an intelligible response to an unliveable situation.

One of the major contemporary exponents of a hermeneutic approach to mental illness is Dorothy Rowe, whose work blends psychiatric critique with self-help. Laing set out to rescue psychosis from the explanatory approach, and to restore intelligibility to the utterances and actions of the 'mad.' One can view Rowe's work in a similar way, but as an interpretative guide specifically to depressed experience. In *Depression: the Way Out of Your Prison* (1983), Rowe addresses a book to those who are depressed, and who, she believes, should be encouraged to understand what they are feeling, and to see it as the outcome of their own active construction of experience. Her opposition to the medicalisation and (scientific, causal) explanation of depression is explicit: 'Depression is not a genetic fault or a mysterious illness which descends on us. It is something which we create for ourselves, and just as we create it, so we can dismantle our creation' (D 13). The medical attitude, though, as Rowe notes, is to classify expressions of despair as one or more co-occurring criteria for 'depression' rather than to attempt to understand how the depressive constructs the world and why:

if you tell a psychiatrist that the worst part of your misery is that you are shut out from God and that you dread life and death because you know you are damned, he will nod sympathetically and note that you are exhibiting one of the symptoms of a depressive illness. Your statement carries the same significance as the red spots in measles. (D 37)

Key to Rowe's exposition is a list of principles which, she argues, underlie the depressive interpretation of the world, and which create self-confirming constructions of experience: for example, the depressive may believe '*I am really bad, evil, valueless, unacceptable to myself and other people*' (D 15), and from this opinion, and into it, may flow other personal dogmas. For example, the depressive may also believe that '*life is terrible and death is worse*' (D 15) – punishment for their innate evil is evident in the workings of the world, and may await them beyond death in actual damnation. Rowe expands her account of the 'genre' of depression in various interesting and surprising ways. Even the depressive experience of time is distorted: the present is evacuated of importance, as one lives 'in the horrendous past, and the hopeless, fearful future and never in the present' (D 56). Like Laing, Rowe uses a mixture of clinical cases, poetry, and biography, to set out a plausible and illuminating account of how an individual's 'mental illness' may in truth merely be a certain way of understanding and constructing experience.

What, then, hinders psychiatrists from exhibiting the same sensitivity as Rowe and Laing? Lucy Johnstone argues convincingly that psychiatrists may be significantly worse than the general population at understanding other people. Psychiatrists, like other doctors, are trained to explain the condition underlying a patient's signs and symptoms in order to prescribe a curative, palliative, or preventative treatment. Simply understanding the patient is not a valued skill, and may even be screened out by the demands of medical training (see UAP 131). Furthermore, points out Johnstone, medical staff adopt unconsciously the medical model so thoroughly that 'the member of staff is no longer aware that she or he is indeed making assumptions, that this view is only one of a number of possible views that she or he might hold' (UAP 207).

As well as the generalised training and indoctrination of psychiatrists, there are also hermeneutic obstacles related to gender, class, and culture. For example, how well can a mostly male profession deal with a problem like anorexia which is far more commonly found in a female population? Most men (body-builders and the like excepted) do not feel the same relation to body size and fat that women do. For women, 'being thin,' notes Johnstone, 'has come to represent not only beauty, success, happiness and acceptance, but also certain *moral* qualities like self-control, strength and diligence. [...] All the qualities that we find least acceptable have been projected onto body fat' (UAP 112). Yet, the largely masculine medical establishment concentrates on removing only the primary sign of anorexia – namely, weight loss. Such treatment, argues Johnstone, fails to find the meaning of the anorexic's actions. Instead, such approaches 'are falling into the same trap as the anorexic herself; they are treating her body as an object, as something separate from her as a person, to be forced into one shape or another without any regard to what this means for the young woman herself' (UAP 113). Similar problems, again with a gendered dimension, arise because of the class bias of medical professionals. How, for example, can a consultant earning at least twice the national average wage, and with a secure professional future, understand how despairing life may be for an unemployed steelworker who has lost money, life-structure, and, above all, his identity? The problem is exacerbated because of gender: as masculine men, neither steelworker nor psychiatrist may have much investment in expressing and understanding feelings. As Johnstone notes, 'men are more likely than women to receive a diagnosis of alcoholism or drug addiction, which can be seen as ways of *blocking out* feelings, in contrast to the more typically female pattern of being *overwhelmed by* feelings'

(UAP 124). The sad result is that 'suicide rates in men have always been higher than in women, and have increased dramatically in recent years' (UAP 124).

This professional inability amongst psychiatrists to understand and comprehend their patients is one of the reasons for the formation of organised groups of the 'mentally ill.' The Hearing Voices Network is a prime example of this phenomenon. It was first formed in 1987, when the Dutch psychiatrist Marius Romme appeared on television with a patient, Patsy Hage, who had asked him to pay serious attention to her experience, rather than merely dismissing it as a (schizophrenic) symptom. Their television appearance revealed a surprising fact: there were a great number of people who both heard voices and who coped well without psychiatric diagnosis or treatment. As well as having the good sense not to discuss their anomalous experiences with medical professionals, these individuals also actively managed and interacted with their voices, and understood them as meaningful phenomena. Romme and his collaborator, Sandra Escher, argue in *Accepting Voices* (1993) that 'the real problem is not so much the hearing of these voices, but rather the inability to cope with them' (AV 8). It is of no help to the voice hearer to call such experience 'schizophrenic,' and to encourage the hearer to regard him- or herself as the passive victim of neurological causality. The Hearing Voices Network therefore allows the 'sufferer' to talk with other voice hearers, to develop ways of coping with their voices if they are troublesome, and, above all, to explore their meaning. As Romme and Escher conclude, there may be a variety of non-psychiatric interpretations of such experience: voices may be 'interpreted as fragmented parts of the self,' or as 'providing guidance through creative dialogue,' or as 'opening channels towards and beyond a higher self' (AV 247). This incomplete list is supplemented by the suggestions of various contributors to *Accepting Voices* as to how voices may be understood (rather than explained): voices may offer companionship or the presence of a deceased relative; they may provide the hearer with a sense of importance and power (as Thomas Szasz has tended to suggest); they may, via harmful instructions, express alienated feelings of depression or self-condemnation; they may be a regressive experience in which boundaries between self and other are distorted (as Laing often hypothesised).

Instead, then, of searching for the underlying cause of 'schizophrenia,' Romme and Escher encourage the discovery of multiple and potentially equally valid meanings.

The Hearing Voices Network now has many groups offering support in various countries (including the United Kingdom). By bringing together voice hearers who insist that their experience is meaningful and should not be stigmatised, the Hearing Voices Network is creating a small political movement. Indeed, the Network may be compared to the gay liberation movement of the 1960s. By increasing the intelligibility of their experience to others, and by organising in groups, voice hearers are beginning to challenge the restriction of their rights consequent upon such psychiatric diagnoses as 'schizophrenia.' In his book *Recovery: An Alien Concept* (1999), Ron Coleman, a recovered voice hearer, and a prominent member of the Hearing Voices Network in the UK, discusses his own experiences and his meetings with other voice hearers. Coleman's psychiatric career began not so much with hearing voices, as with drinking to blot them out. After losing his job and home, he eventually encountered a psychiatrist, and was soon 'sectioned' (involuntarily detained under various sections of mental health legislation) and medicated without his consent. So began a ten-year spell as a psychiatric patient suffering from 'schizophrenia.' What is extraordinary in Coleman's story is the idiocy of the profession that looked after him. Prominent amongst Coleman's voices was that of the parish priest who had abused him as a child, and also the voice of his first love, who had committed suicide without warning or explanation. No-one sought to ask Coleman the meaning of his experiences: how he had felt, what the voices told him, and so forth – until, that is, he was put in touch with a group of voice-hearers. When Coleman first attended a Hearing Voices group, he was asked '*Do you hear voices?*' and when he confirmed that he did, he was told '*They are real you know*' (RAC 59). To a certain kind of medical mind, this remark would seem merely to be confirming Coleman's delusions. But, of course, 'real' in this sense does not mean that a disembodied voice *really is* echoing through the air, disturbing all and sundry. Rather, 'real' means existentially, humanly real: the experience has a meaning and a significance of its own; it is not mere random noise, like seeing stars after being knocked on the head. Of course, were voice hearers thoroughly medicalised, and rigorously 'treated,' the

Hearing Voices Network could never have come into being. We are back again at the point made earlier: a civilised society must allow 'loopholes' for deviance to occur. The more efficiently 'illness' is detected and treated by eagle-eyed GPs and their allies, the less likely it is that challenges such as the Hearing Voices Network can arise.

An important point should also be made: the Hearing Voices Network is operating precisely within that Laingian paradigm which I have already described. Philip Thomas in *The Dialectics of Schizophrenia* (1997) discusses the Network, pointing out that 'the explanatory framework used by most psychiatrists renders them incapable of exploring their patients' experiences;' consequently, though 'we might be able to provide a detailed cognitive or neuropsychological explanation of voices,' 'this would be meaningless to the person who had the experiences' (DOS 190). This is exactly Laing's position regarding psychosis in *The Divided Self*: an explanation of such an experience as hearing voices immediately evacuates it of meaning. One must firstly ask, charitably and sympathetically, if such experiences can indeed be understood, rather than dismissed, to use Thomas's apt phrase, as 'the meaningless noise of disordered neurones' (DOS 181). This is unlikely to be accomplished without sensitive and detailed communication with voice hearers. Thomas also echoes another of Laing's cautions, for he notes that 'we must beware of the dangers of reinterpreting the experience, which, to my mind, is the flaw of psychoanalytic models' (DOS 191). This too was a warning made by Laing in *The Divided Self*: if we immediately interpret psycho-analytically, rather than understand hermeneutically, then we again risk obscuring, rather than clarifying, the meaning of an experience for the person who has it. We shall search, via endless psychoanalytic transformations, for the laws of psychic development underlying the utterances of the 'patient.'

Conclusion

Critical psychiatry has raised many sceptical questions that must be answered before one can justifiably apply a medical model to 'mental illness.' Do patients have the right to remain deviant?; are they really a threat to themselves or others, or are they just unusual? Even if someone insists on being treated as 'sick' should society in fact accede to this request? Suppose that the ascription of deviance is legitimate: the person is harming themselves or others, for example. Is the patient's condition intelligible and meaningful, and would psycho-spiritual therapies be effective? Even, of course, if we can draw out no such intelligibility, a doubt must remain: we, the interlocutors, may simply be too clumsy to transpose ourselves into the patient's experience – this was the limitation that led to the formation of self-help groups such as Hearing Voices. Assume, though, that these doubts have been eliminated, or that urgent pressures compel action. If we are indeed to offer a biopsychiatric treatment then we must be sure that we are faced with an appropriate disorder: namely, a rigorously defined organic condition which is susceptible to chemical, surgical, or other intervention with acceptable side-effects, and significant alleviation consequent upon treatment.

The efforts of the anti-psychiatrists have not been in vain – despite Laing's pessimism about the fate of his ideas. Dedicated researchers, and those with first-hand of experience of so-called 'mental illness,' have banded together to assert the rights, and to promote the intelligibility, of those who might be on the receiving end of psychiatric diagnosis and treatment. Though the critical psychiatrists are perhaps less colourful than their antipsychiatric predecessors, they have the virtues of persistence and discipline. With enough time and pressure, the critical psychiatrists may yet compel the 'caring' professions to examine the assumptions which are too often made unthinkingly about what is in the interests of the 'patient.'

Conclusion

I introduced this book with the thought that the work of R.D. Laing was unjustly neglected, and that this unfair treatment was especially manifest in, of all places, his native country. For various reasons – cultural, political, and institutional – Laing's work has not received its due recognition in Scotland. One of the primary aims of this book is to put the record straight. By largely bypassing Laing's personal life, I have moved straight to the heart of the matter – his ideas in their national and international context. I have tried, in the main, to provide a charitable interpretation of Laing's work. It seems to me that the most vital task is simply to show the logic and meaning of Laing's ideas in order to rescue them from their widespread misinterpretation (a consequence of inattentive and selective quotation from his weakest writings).

There can be little doubt, though, that there are justified criticisms of Laing's ideas (rather than of the man or his mythology). That Laing romanticised 'schizophrenia' and psychic regression is widely accepted. Daniel Burston in *The Crucible of Experience* (2000) provides the most balanced and intelligent commentary. Yet his conclusion is unequivocal: 'If the question is whether Laing ever, at any time, romanticized schizophrenia, *despite the suffering it entails*, the answer, unfortunately, is "yes." From 1964 to 1969, Laing was "over the top," despite later disclaimers to the contrary' (CE 71) – this was the period in which Laing assumed too readily that all psychotic breakdowns could involve a process of spiritual rebirth. This obsession with birth and rebirth intensified in the later period where Laing developed various extraordinary hypotheses on how uterine experience could affect the course of one's entire life. These involved, as Burston notes, attributing 'a dim awareness of the mother's attitude and intentions to a zygote prior to implantation in the uterine wall, some eight months before a normal birth,' and then a subsequent hypothesis that 'self/world schemata acquired *prior* to birth have a more formative and lingering influence [...] than events occurring postpartum' (CE 51).

However, beyond these clear failures of evidence and argument, the remainder of Laing's work is remarkably cogent. Of course, there is always the threat of argument *ad hominem* that Laing's ideas are wrong because of all the foolish, unpleasant and selfish things that he did.

There can be little doubt that meeting Laing when he was in the wrong mood could be a deeply unpleasant experience; there is also little doubt that Laing's extraordinary empathic plasticity – the ease with which he could understand the psychotic worldview, for example – was a (useful) side-effect of his own personal difficulties. Laing's ideas, though, stand or fall on their own merits.

There is an additional reason why Laing is so rarely given his due: he lacks allies in the other movements which profited from 1960s counter-culture. The feminist scholar Elaine Showalter, for example, is quite scathing of Laing in *The Female Malady* (1987). In this work, unfortunately subtitled *Women, Madness, and English* [sic] *Culture, 1830–1980*, she refers to Laing's therapeutic relation as that of a self-styled 'manly physician-priest leading another explorer to the heart of darkness' (FM 236). While acknowledging Laing's usefulness for feminist thought, Showalter still aligns him with therapists who ignore or exploit their female patients. She writes that Laing, faced with a Kingsley Hall resident such as Mary Barnes who underwent a prolonged regression, was met with 'an obligation to play mother' at odds with his 'own heroic fantasies' based on 'a male adventure of exploration and conquest' (FM 236). Laing, when these criticisms were put to him by Bob Mullan, responded with a convincing argument: 'I've never made anything out of Mary Barnes. I've never used her as an example or a paradigm case or set her up in anything I've written or in lectures I've given' (MTBN 185). Indeed, Laing was not even Barnes's therapist; despite Showalter's claim that 'Mary Barnes is in fact Laing's only complete case study, his Augustine, his Dora, his Anna O' (FM 232), her principal therapist was Joseph Berke. Showalter's tactic is familiar: it is guilt by association – by associating with Berke or David Cooper, Laing is necessarily implicated in their beliefs and therapeutic style.

I suspect that Showalter's criticisms are motivated by a dislike for Laing as a person. Laing, indeed, could hardly be called a 'new man:' abandoning his wife and family does not epitomise fatherly responsibility. And, though he was comfortable with children and fathered ten of his own, he was, as he remarked in interview, 'a Scottish male chauvinist pig who has got very little time for the business of changing the nappies of babies' (MTBN 322). Yet, *contra* Showalter, surprisingly little of this confessed failing spills over into his published work or therapeutic practices. Like Masson twenty years later, Laing too observed the sexism of Freud during his encounter with Dora, the young woman who was a pawn in the relationship between her father, his mistress, and the latter's husband (see WM 209). Laing was also unlikely to bamboozle suffering women by demanding therapeutic 'insight' instead of practical action. In his interviews with Mullan, Laing tells a tale of domestic abuse:

One woman, who was living with her father who for years had been in the habit of beating her up, I said, 'I mean *you* haven't got a problem.' 'But I can't even lift the phone up,' well, I said, phone up someone. 'When you walk out of here, we will get a car to come round and pick you up in 20 minutes and you just go and stay with that person. Don't go back into that house, that's the end of it, right? OK, so do that.' [...] I said just get out of it, and when the dust has settled and you are able to calm down you'll be able to see what you've been living in. (MTBN 322)

A certain kind of psychotherapist at the time might have dealt with this case in another way: firstly, the woman would have to undergo a transference relation in which she worked through the issues underlying her domestic relationship, and in which, presumably, her position in the abusive household would eventually be revealed as a masochistic dependency which expressed an unconscious guilt at her incestuous fixation on her father. This would be a classic instance of psychoanalytic oppressiveness: the problem is the woman's, and the only way she can escape it is by dealing with her sexual attraction to the man who abuses her. Laing, to his feminist credit, cuts the Gordian knot by insisting on action *before* insight. Why this woman stuck out this situation can be sorted out another day; what is important is that she first frees herself by her own choice. Rather than assenting to the therapeutic assumption that she is the victim of psychological causality, he invites this woman to experience her own existential freedom (with, of course, due support from others, rather than a mere abstract demand that she 'choose radically').

Laing was also capable of feminist statements at a theoretical level. In *The Voice of Experience*, he returns again to the human agency which is required in order to understand the world scientifically, and yet which itself eludes scientific analysis: 'non-objective acts create objectivity. [...] the "objective" world comes into view only when we are objective.

Nothing is more subjective than objectivity blind to its subjectivity' (VE 17). This blindness arises because although 'the scientific look is an *act*,' this '*act* is not one of the facts his [the scientist's] look brings into view' (VE 22). The gender of Laing's pronoun is not accidental. He directly links the objectifying gaze of the scientist with a 'scientific programme of unbridled male domination' in which nature is 'a woman for us to look over, strip and do with as we will' (VE 21). This is a thought that should warm the heart of any contemporary 'postmodern' feminist: Laing genders the distinction between explanation and understanding, and implies that motivating the former there is something akin to masculine sexuality. Whatever Laing's personal failings, as a therapist and as an intellectual he was broadly sympathetic to feminist thoughts and principles.

Some assistance from feminists would be useful to those who follow Laing's legacy. Feminist critiques of the objectifying techniques of science might help to counter the widespread assumption that developments in biological psychiatry have 'disproven' Laing's ideas. To a large extent, biopsychiatric advances (howsoever plausible) are largely beside the point; and where biopsychiatrists do attempt to discuss the work of Laing and others, they tend to misrepresent the ideas with which they engage. These points I dealt with in the previous chapter, but they are still worth summarising. The misguided attempt by medics to implicate anti- and critical psychiatry in mind-body dualism indicates their inability to engage properly with the debate. Whether or not mind and body are separate substances, medical diagnosis – both physical and mental – is essentially normative. One works to eliminate, alleviate, or prevent certain undesirable human conditions. Without human desires and values, there simply is no such thing as illness (just as Sartre once remarked that, without humans to witness it, destruction is merely the meaningless rearrangement of matter). Misled by the relative stability of norms of health, the medical profession can – for most intents and purposes – overlook the social construction of illness. Problems begin when this reifying attitude is unwittingly carried over into 'mental health.' Culture is frozen into nature: homosexuality becomes a disease (until gays fight back); hearing voices is converted into an unintelligible neurological chaos; depression is no more than a chemical imbalance. When the 'mentally ill' are deprived of liberty and intelligibility, then medicine is free to deduce cures from the crudest of 'treatments.' This procedure is fallible enough with physical disease: aspirin, for example, reveals little about the aetiology of the common cold. It is especially reprehensible when the treatment is directed at deviant experience. At least in the old days, psychiatric violence was obvious. Hitting somebody on the head with a club kept them quiet, but no one was foolish enough to postulate a deficit in cranial trauma which could be treated by introductions of kinetic energy ('concussion therapy,' as it were).

Perhaps what is most offensive to medical psychiatry is Laing's interpretive method, an approach to therapy which works against unifying hypotheses like those proposed by the natural sciences. Laing's technique is also a challenge to traditional psychiatric 'interpretation' where a one-sided understanding provides some specious confirmation for the 'laws' of the psyche. Laing's method and its results are shown to best effect in *The Divided Self*, which will probably stand as his greatest work. Furthermore, by taking adult personal relationships as psychoanalytically significant, Laing moved beyond both traditional Freudian psychiatry and the object-relations perspective developed by Fairbairn and others. The results of his interpersonal and interpretative method are well shown in *Sanity, Madness, and the Family*, where seemingly unintelligible behaviour becomes understandable when seen in its social context.

Like other philosophers and psychiatrists influenced by 'Continental' thought, Laing operated a distinction between 'explanation' and 'understanding.' Unlike them, however, he usually wrote in a clear and engaging prose style, and generally avoided the repetition of abstract mantras, or the construction of weighty arguments without illustration and justification. He should be congratulated for this: he did not try to imitate a 'scientific' prose style, where endless Latinate jargon and a tedious use of the passive voice mimic writing in the natural sciences. Laing's stylistic clarity renders his relative obscurity all the more unfortunate. As Laing points out to Bob Mullan, 'I haven't gone out of my way to marginalise my writing as eccentric in any way. In fact, very much the opposite – of trying to use ordinary words in an ordinary way and ordinary syntax and say as simply and clearly as I can what I intend to say' (MTBN 337). There would indeed be something contradictory if Laing tried to emulate a scientific way of writing, where the passivity of the prose concentrates the mind on the (hypothetical) universal processes that are recorded under experimental conditions (conditions which, though, are created by the agency of the 'observer'). To Laing, the activities of human beings as they attempt to understand each other are vital to his exegesis of personal experience; why on earth would he try to write as if personal agency were irrelevant?

At the very least, Laing should be thought of as a great Scottish writer. He was not often a creative writer, though his work does contain poetic and imaginative passages, and he was required – like other psychiatrists – to fictionalise his case studies sufficiently to preserve client confidentiality. Yet, even in their non-fictional aspects, his writings are admirable enough to become canonical Scottish literature. The acclaimed contemporary Scots poet, Tom Leonard, sees Laing as a writer with both a European and a Scottish heritage. *The Divided Self*, believes Leonard, ranks alongside 'Kierkegaard's *Either-Or*, Beckett's novels, Sartre's *Nausea*, Robbe-Grillet, Gabriel Marcel's *Being and Having*' (CD 90); yet, points out Leonard, 'you can think about Laing in relation to Robert Owen's New Lanark [a nineteenth-century model community], to Alasdair Gray's [novel] *Lanark*, to [the artist] Ian Hamilton Finlay's garden at Stonypath,' and also to James Thomson's long poem *'The City of Dreadful Night'* (CD 91). Leonard's own work uses a spelling that attempts to convey working-class Scots pronunciation – this is part of his deliberate strategy to highlight the assumed naturalness and superiority of Standard English (the variety spoken by the upper-middle classes in the South of England). In Leonard's opinion, 'What Laing got to the heart of was the nature of complicity in relationships within institutional structures, and the creation of supposedly self-invalidating "otherness" in people who do not "speak the right language"' (CD 90). Leonard therefore sees a parallel between his own poetry and Laing's ideas: both he and Laing attempt to restore dignity and intelligibility to those who are invalidated and demeaned because (in the broadest sense) of the way they communicate.

Laing's work, I believe, provides much that is of enduring intellectual and spiritual value – that is, at least, once one penetrates what Leonard has called the 'smokescreen anecdotage about Laing being drunk, presenting him as a boozer and a druggie, and therefore a poser' (CD 91). Like any other person, Laing had his failings, but his ideas on the theory of psychiatry, the meaning and reality of mental illness, the role of interpersonal relations, and transcendent experience, continue to inspire and provoke. Given today's psychiatric culture, which is infatuated with a biomedical approach, Laing's work is all the more valuable. Furthermore, outside of his contribution to psychiatry, Laing also discusses problems (such as explanation and understanding, and the 'divided self') which illuminate complex philosophical issues. This philosophical element – that 'democratic intellect' which shines through in Laing's writings – points to a neglected history of ideas in Scotland. Laing is the tip of an iceberg; behind and around him stand other thinkers such as William Robertson Smith, Ian Suttie, W.R.D. Fairbairn, John Macmurray, Maxwell Jones, and A.S. Neill.

Bibliography

Baillie, J.B., *Studies in Human Nature* (London: Bell, 1921)

Beveridge, Craig and Ronald Turnbull, *The Eclipse of Scottish Culture: Inferiorism and the Intellectuals* (Edinburgh: Polygon, 1989)

Boyle, Mary, *Schizophrenia: A Scientific Delusion?* (London: Routledge, 1990)

Breggin, Peter R., *Toxic Psychiatry: Drugs and Electroconvulsive Therapy: The Truth and Better Alternatives* (London: HarperCollins, 1993)

Bultmann, Rudolf, 'The Problem of Hermeneutics' in *Essays: Philosophical and Theological*, trans. by James C.G. Greig (London: SCM, 1955), pp.234–61

Burston, Daniel, *The Crucible of Experience: R.D. Laing and the Crisis of Psychotherapy* (Cambridge, Mass. and London: Harvard, 2000)

Burston, Daniel, *The Wing of Madness: The Life and Work of R.D. Laing* (Cambridge, Mass. and London: Harvard, 1996)

Clay, John, *R.D. Laing: A Divided Self: A Biography* (London: Hodder and Stoughton, 1997)

Coleman, Ron, *Recovery: An Alien Concept* (Gloucester: Handsell, 1999)

Cooper, David, *Psychiatry and Anti-Psychiatry* (London: Granada, 1970)

Cooper, David, *The Grammar of Living: An Examination of Political Acts* (London: Allen Lane, 1974)

Cooper, David, *The Language of Madness* (Harmondsworth: Penguin, 1980)

Costello, John E., *John Macmurray: A Biography* (Floris: Edinburgh, 2002)

Davie, George Elder, *The Democratic Intellect: Scotland and her Universities in the Nineteenth Century*, 2nd edn (Edinburgh: Edinburgh University Press, 1964)

Descartes, René, 'Discourse on the Method of Rightly Conducting the Reason', in *The Philosophical Works of Descartes*, trans. by Elizabeth S. Haldane and G.R.T. Ross, 2 vols (Cambridge: Cambridge University, 1911), I, pp.81–130

Diagnostic and Statistical Manual of Mental Disorders, 4th edn (Washington, DC: American Psychiatric Association, 1994)

Fairbairn, W. Ronald D., 'A Revised Psychopathology of the Psychoses and Neuroses', in W. Ronald D. Fairbairn, *Psychoanalytic Studies of the Personality* (London: Tavistock, 1952), pp.28–58

Fairbairn, W. Ronald D., 'Schizoid Factors in the Personality', in W. Ronald D. Fairbairn, *Psychoanalytic Studies of the Personality* (London: Tavistock, 1952), pp.3–27

Fairbairn, W. Ronald D., 'The Treatment and Rehabilitation of Sexual Offenders' in W. Ronald D. Fairbairn, *Psychoanalytic Studies of the Personality* (London: Tavistock, 1952), pp.289–96

Fairbairn, W. Ronald D., 'The War Neuroses – Their Nature and Significance' in W. Ronald D. Fairbairn, *Psychoanalytic Studies of the Personality* (London: Tavistock, 1952), pp.256–88

Fairbairn,W.R.D., 'Reevaluating Some Basic Concepts' in W.R.D. Fairbairn, *From Instinct to Self: Selected Papers of W.R.D. Fairbairn Volume 1: Clinical and Theoretical Papers*, ed. David E. Scharff and Ellinor Fairbairn Birtles (Northvale, New Jersey; London: Jason Aronson, 1994), I, pp.129–38

Foucault, Michel, *Madness and Civilization: a History of Insanity in the Age of Reason*, trans. by Richard Howard (London: Routledge, 1989)

Goffman, Erving, *Asylums: Essays in the Social Situation of Mental Patients and Other Inmates* (Harmondsworth: Penguin, 1968)

Goffman, Erving, 'The Insanity of Place' in *Psychiatry*, 32:4 (1969), pp.357–88

Goffman, Erving, *The Presentation of Self in Everyday Life* (Harmondsworth: Penguin, 1971)

Heard, Dorothy, 'Introduction: Historical Perspectives' in Ian D. Suttie, *The Origins of Love and Hate* (London: Free Association, 1988), pp.xix–xl

Heller, Joseph, *Catch-22* (New York: Simon & Schuster, 1994)

Howe, Gwen, *The Reality of Schizophrenia* (London: Faber and Faber, 1991)

Howe, Gwen, *Working with Schizophrenia: A Needs Based Approach* (London: Jessica Kingsley, 1995)

Hughes, Judith M., *Reshaping the Psychoanalytic Domain: The Work of Melanie Klein, W.R.D. Fairbairn, and D.W. Winnicott* (Berkeley and Los Angeles, California; London: University of California Press, 1989)

Hume, David, *A Treatise of Human Nature*, ed. by L.A. Selby-Bigge, 2nd edn (Oxford: Clarendon, 1978)

Jaspers, Karl, *General Psychopathology*, trans. by J. Hoeing and Marian W. Hamilton (Manchester: Manchester University, 1963)

Jenner, F.A., 'On the Legacy of Ronald Laing' in *Janus Head: Journal of Interdisciplinary Studies in Literature, Continental Philosophy, Phenomenological Psychiatry, and the Arts*, 4.1 (2001), pp.90–101

Johnstone, Lucy, *Users and Abusers of Psychiatry: A Critical Look at Psychiatric Practice* 2nd edn (London: Routledge, 2000)

Jones, Maxwell, *The Process of Change* (London: Routledge and Kegan Paul, 1982)

Kotowiecz, Zbigniew, *R.D. Laing and the Paths of Anti-Psychiatry* (London: Routledge, 1997)

Kutchings, Herb and Stuart A. Kirk, *Making Us Crazy: DSM: The Psychiatric Bible and the Creation of Mental Disorders* (London: Constable, 1999)

Laing, Adrian C., *R.D. Laing: A Biography* (London: Harper Collins, 1997)

Laing, R.D., *The Divided Self: An Existential Study in Sanity and Madness* (Harmondsworth, Middlesex: Pelican, 1965)

Laing, R.D., *The Facts of Life* (Penguin: London, 1976)

Laing, R.D. *Knots* (London: Tavistock, 1970)

Laing, R.D., *The Politics of Experience and the Bird of Paradise* (London: Penguin, 1967)

Laing, R.D., 'The Politics of the Family' in R.D. Laing, *The Politics of the Family and Other Essays* (London: Tavistock, 1971), pp.65–124

Laing, R.D., *Sanity, Madness and the Family: Volume I: Families of Schizophrenics* (London: Tavistock, 1964)

Laing, R.D., *The Self and Others: Further Studies in Sanity and Madness* (London: Tavistock, 1961)

Laing, R.D., *The Voice of Experience* (Allen Lane, Penguin: London, 1982)

Laing, R.D., *Wisdom, Madness, and Folly: The Making of a Psychiatrist 1927–57*, Canongate Classics 89 (Edinburgh: Canongate, 1998)

Laing, R.D. and D.G. Cooper, *Reason and Violence: a Decade of Sartre's Philosophy*, 2nd edn (London: Tavistock, 1971)

Laing, R.D., H. Phillipson and A.R. Lee, *Interpersonal Perception: a Theory and a Method of Research* (London and New York: Tavistock and Springer, 1966)

Lifton, R., '"Thought Reform" of Western Civilians in Chinese Communist Prisons' in *Psychiatry*, 19:2 (1956), pp.173–95

Macmurray, John, *The Boundaries of Science: A Study in the Philosophy of Psychology* (London: Faber, 1939)

Macmurray, John, *Interpreting the Universe* (London: Faber and Faber, 1933)

Macmurray, John, *Persons in Relation being the Gifford Lectures delivered in the University of Glasgow in 1954 by John Macmurray* (London: Faber and Faber, 1961)

Macmurray, John, *The Self as Agent: being the Gifford Lectures delivered in the University of Glasgow in 1953 by John Macmurray* (London: Faber and Faber, 1957)

Masson, Jeffrey, *Against Therapy: Warning: Psychotherapy May Be Hazardous to your Mental Health* (London: Collins, 1989)

Mullan, Bob, *Mad to be Normal: Conversations with R.D. Laing* (London: Free Association, 1995)

Mullan, Bob, *R.D. Laing: A Personal View* (London: Duckworth, 1999)

R.D. Laing: Creative Destroyer, ed. by Bob Mullan (London: Cassell, 1997)

Reich, Wilhelm, *The Function of the Orgasm: Sex-Economic Problems of Biological Energy*, trans. Vincent R. Carfagno (London: Souvenir, 1983)

Reich, Wilhelm, and A.S. Neill, *Record of a Friendship: The Correspondence Between Wilhelm Reich and A.S. Neill 1936–1957*, ed. by Beverley R. Placzek (London: Gollancz, 1982)

Romme, Marius and Sandra Escher, *Accepting Voices* (London: Mind, 1993)

Roth, Martin and Jerome Kroll, *The Reality of Mental Illness* (Cambridge: Cambridge University, 1986)

Rowe, Dorothy, *Depression: The Way out of your Prison* (London: Routledge and Kegan Paul, 1983)

Scharff, David E. and Ellinor Fairbairn Birtles, 'Editor's Introduction: Fairbairn's Contribution', in *From Instinct to Self: Selected Papers of W.R.D. Fairbairn Volume 1: Clinical and Theoretical Papers*, 2 vols, Scharff, David E. and Ellinor Fairbairn Birtles (eds.) (Northvale, New Jersey; London, England: Jason Aronson, 1994), I, pp.xi–xxi

Scheff, Thomas J., *Being Mentally Ill: A Sociological Theory* (Chicago: Aldine, 1966)

Sedgwick, Peter, *Psycho Politics* (London: Pluto, 1982)

Showalter, Elaine, *The Female Malady* (London: Virago, 1987)

Smith, W. Robertson, *Lectures on the Religion of the Semites: First Series: The Fundamental Institutions*, new edn (London: Adam and Charles Black, 1894)

Sutherland, J.D., *Fairbairn's Journey into the Interior* (London: Free Association, 1989)

Suttie, Ian D., *The Origins of Love and Hate* (London: Kegan Paul, 1935)

Szasz, Thomas, *The Myth of Mental Illness: Foundations of a Theory of Personal Conduct* (London: Secker & Warburg, 1962)

Szasz, Thomas, *Ideology and Insanity: Essays on the Psychiatric Dehumanization of Man* (London: Calder and Boyars, 1973)

Szasz, Thomas, *The Second Sin* (London: Routledge and Kegan Paul, 1974)

Szasz, Thomas, 'Anti-psychiatry: the Paradigm of the Plundered Mind' in *New Review* 3:29 (1976), pp.3–14

Szasz, Thomas, *Insanity: The Idea and its Consequences* (New York: John Wiley, 1987)

Tarsis, Valeriy, *Ward 7: an autobiographical novel*, trans. by Katya Brown (London and Glasgow: Collins and Harvill, 1965)

Thomas, Philip, *The Dialectics of Schizophrenia* (London: Free Association, 1997)

Vonnegut, Kurt, *Slaughterhouse-Five or The Children's Crusade: A Duty-Dance with Death* (London: Vintage, 1991)

Index of Names